YO-BTI-553

HUB BUB

The Hubbub Guide to Cycling

by Diane Lingelbach

© 1997. All rights reserved.

DEDICATION

This book is dedicated to my husband, Jon. He gave me the idea, and then he left me alone to pursue it. He gave me the support by leaving the house almost every day and not complaining when he got home because nothing else got done. And, most importantly, he gave me the freedom and space to be as nuts as I am. I love him to pieces!

I need to thank some people...beginning with my childhood friend Paul Bernheimer, who knew instinctively what I wanted the finished book to look like and executed it, with absolute perfection. A huge thanks to Carolyn Kottler for her inspired thinking that resulted in the HUBBUB name and to Phyllis Day for her bright and forthright editing and proofreading, and to my daughter and niece Sydney and Rachael, who put up with me all summer while I sat at the keyboard and ignored everything else!

THANKS – YOU GUYS!

CONTENTS

© All contents copyright DBL Promotions, Inc. 1997.

HUB BUB

INTRODUCTION
The Absolutely, Positively, Best Information Available Anywhere About How To Take A Bicycle Vacation And Other Related Bicycle Stuff.... No Lie!

So, what will it take to get you to READ this compendium of information? You must have some interest in cycling - and especially in cycle-touring, or else why would you be holding this in your hands?

We promise that IF you read this, there will be information that will help you to ride for longer periods of time and keep you comfortable while on that skinny little thing they call a saddle. We will suggest simple positioning changes so that your hands, fingers, and private parts won't fall asleep and your shoulders, neck, and back won't feel as if you have been run over by a Mack truck - with chains!

We will help you through the what to take, what to wear, and what to do process. We believe there are no stupid questions, so if at any time, you cannot find an answer to something that puzzles you, we urge you to call, write, email, or fax us.

How do we know all these weird and peculiar things, you ask? Well, our uncommon perspective on bicycle touring comes from more than twenty years in bicycle retail. We have equipped people for three day leisure touring in New England and two month journeys across Canada and Alaska. We have sent three women on a round-the-world cycling-hiking trip and are now monitoring a good friend's two year bicycling odyssey to document how other cultures use their resources and maintain sustainability.

We believe that cycle-touring is an incredible way to see the world - just about any part of it! The at-your-own-speed pace, the method of movement, the ability to stop and truly "smell the flowers," all help make traveling by bicycle a joy. At the end of a day of sightseeing-by-bike, you will feel so very good about yourself and what you have accomplished!

Our interests are in seeing people enjoy, find, and stretch themselves using a bicycle as the means to those ends. We really do care that your commitment to a cycle tour for the only two or three weeks of vacation you get a year, should be the BEST two or three weeks you experience.

We hope that this compilation of important, obscure, sometimes enlightening, and occasionally irrelevant facts will teach you something you might not have already known and might even make you laugh once or twice. What we cannot do for you is get you out on your bike and begin the pedaling that will get you in shape for your adventure - THAT you will have to motivate yourself to do. Happy riding!

Oh, one last comment (you thought we'd let you off that easily?) - You most certainly do NOT have to be a world-class athlete to take a bicycle tour. In fact, most people who decide to try an adventure cycling vacation have never been on an extended ride of this sort.

**Write us:
HubBub, 2124 Lee Rd,
Cleveland Heights, Ohio
44118**

Call us: 1-800-888-2027

Fax us at (216) 371-5289

**Email us:
HubBub@ibm.net**

**Visit our Website:
http://www.hubbub.com**

You can find most of the products we mention in our HUBBUB Cycling Catalog. It's free for the asking

WHERE ARE WE GOING?
("I Thought YOU Knew!")

In our ongoing research into cycle-touring, we have seen the number of tour companies literally explode! There are dozens and dozens of companies that offer cycling trips anywhere and everywhere in the world. Some companies offer luxury tours, others are geared toward a more moderate price range. Some cater to a mature cyclist, others are more youth oriented. Because there are not very many travel agents who specialize in bicycle adventures, finding the right tour company might seem like a daunting task.

Here are some basic questions to help begin your search and qualify a specific touring company:

Where do you want to go? Do you want to see a special part of the U.S, or have you always wanted to ride through Provence? Take into consideration the lay of the land - flat, hilly, MOUNTAINOUS! and the amount of time you have for your adventure.

What are your riding abilities? Do you want to ride 35-50 leisurely miles per day and spend a lot of time sightseeing or are you expecting to ride longer distances in a challenging environment? (You can even follow the 2,000+ mile Tour de France route.)

What time of year will you be traveling? And, to what type of climate? Vermont is lovely in the Fall; Australia is warm in December. The desert will be cold early mornings and hot midday. Ireland has

been known to have nasty summers with cold weather and rain week after week. Especially if you have to reserve your vacation times long in advance, you will want to know the weather probabilities for any given destination.

In what type of accommodations do you want to stay? Bed-and-breakfasts in Virginia are quaint and lovely, often moderately priced. A 5-star hotel most likely has round-the-clock room service and will accommodate your every whim.

How many days do you want to spend riding? Most tour companies offer set itineraries - 3-day, 5-day, 7-day, etc. Although custom tours are often available. Don't forget to leave some non-riding days for sightseeing or just some R&R.

How much do you want to spend on your tour? Bear in mind that airfare, accommodations prior to and just after your trip, and ground transportation are not usually included. Bicycle rental may also be additional... we'll talk more about that later.

How many other guests would you like on your tour? Intimate tours may have as few as 6 or 8 guests while the party-on-the-road type of ride could be dozens, hundreds, even thousands. You will meet wonderful people on a bicycle tour no matter what the size.

Do you have dietary restrictions or considerations? If you keep Kosher or are a vegetarian, you don't want to end up on a tour with pork and beef. You get the picture. Ask.

Finally, write down all those nagging little questions - that's what we're here for. While we are not recommending any particular touring company, we can answer your questions or find out the answers for you. Write, email, fax, or phone us!

The Vehicle
64 Spokes, 2 Wheels, 21 Gears, 2 Brakes....
(Oh Noooooo!)

Quick Tip: - A bicycle is going to be your best friend by the time you are ready for your trip.

For the novice rider, the bicycle itself is perhaps the most intimidating aspect of the experience Well, we are here to tell you - NO SWEAT! The key to a great cycling experience is the FIT of the bicycle - When you are comfortable, you will be able to ride longer, at a faster pace, and with more enjoyment. At the end of the day, you will still be able to relish your dinner, do some sightseeing, get a great night's rest and be ready and eager to ride the next day.

TAKE MY OWN OR RENT???? (will that be paper or plastic?)

Most touring companies offer bicycle rental as part of their services. Especially when traveling abroad, we highly recommend renting a bicycle for your tour. If you are traveling by car to your start destination and are more comfortable with your own bike by all means, take it along. If your decision is to take your bike and you need to ship it - here are some guidelines.

• Be certain that your bike is in excellent mechanical condition when you leave.

• Try to find enough time to send it on ahead to a reputable Professional Bicycle Dealer for last minute reassembly and a quick checkover or;

• Have the appropriate tools to reassemble it on

site when you get to your destination (long handled pedal wrench and allen wrenches at the minimum)

• Remember to insure your bike for its REPLACEMENT value.

• Make good arrangements for the safekeeping of the box or crate in which you shipped your bike for your return trip home.

NOPE, I'LL RENT ONE OF THEIRS, Thanks...

When you choose to rent one of the touring company bikes, you will be asked several things about the bicycle you will be riding during your tour. As a rule, there are printed guidelines from the touring company to help in choosing the size and type of bicycle for the trip you have planned.

(See Metric Conversion Chart in Chapter 18)

ALL THIS NEW-FANGLED GEARing!

If your experience of a bicycle with multiple gears was one of a constant hassle - chain falling off, grinding of gears, and missed shifts - don't fret! The shifting on all new bicycles is absolutely fool-proof. Referred to as "indexed shifting," each gear "clicks" into position with a positive sound. You are able to change gears under almost any condition because of today's modern shifting systems.

Most of the tour company rental bikes will also be equipped with one or two water bottles, a rear rack and perhaps a handlebar bag. If you need space for a camera or other on-the-road equipment, we discuss other small packs in the Amenities section. We do NOT recommend backpacks.

Here is a run down on the 3 types of bicycles you might be offered on tour.

HYBRID BICYCLES

For today's average cycle-tour, i.e. 3-10 days, flat to rolling hills, 35-50 miles per day - most companies offer a man's or lady's "hybrid" bicycle for their guests. This bicycle has a fairly wide but smooth treaded tire which gives you a stable and easy-rolling ride. The handlebars are upright with either a slight rise or a straight-across configuration. You are not "bent over" in the classic 10-speed "racer" position. Hybrids are fairly lightweight and easy to pedal.

The hybrid bicycle probably has 21 gears. NOW DON'T PANIC! We've already explained how foolproof the shifting is. Think of your gears this way - you have 7 high gears for downhill and straight-away riding (yeeee-haaaa); 7 gears for slightly rolling hills, and 7 BAIL-ME-OUT-I-DON'T-WANT-TO-GET-OFF-AND-WALK hill-climbing gears. With these choices you should be able to pedal at the same rate of speed under all road conditions. (That is precisely the point of all the gears!)

MOUNTAIN BIKES

If you are taking an off-road tour, or a bicycle adventure with poorly defined roads, you will probably be offered a mountain bike. This bike also has at least 21 gears (some of the newer systems offer 24,) but they are mostly hill-climbing and slow-speed gears. In off-road riding, travel speeds are relatively slow and the terrain frequently uneven. The handlebars will be straight-across, although a "bar-end" may be added for an extra hand position. Bar-ends can be very helpful for "pulling" uphill.

The mountain bike is very stable and is intended for steep ascents and descents over crudely surfaced roads or trails. Mountain bikes are sometimes outfitted with smooth tires and used for touring situations. They are still mountain bikes in terms of the gearing and geometry however and will not perform as well on road as a hybrid or touring bicycle. Which brings us to the last category.

CLASSIC TOURING BICYCLES

Many companies still offer what we would call traditional "touring" bikes. These bicycles do have the conventional "10-speed" handlebars which result in a "bent over" or aerodynamic position, 21-24 gears, very narrow tires, and are designed to go much faster than hybrids or mountain bikes. Touring bicycles are not quite as stable as hybrids - you sacrifice some of that stability for speed. Touring bicycles are considerably more stable than racing bicycles, however.

While riding a touring bike, your upper body placement and multiple position handlebars allow for more places to put your hands. This in turn gives you the ability to move your hands around and avoid fatigue resulting from the one-position grip of a straight across bar. When fitted appropriately, the aerodynamic, racer-style position can become quite comfortable. Also, the more experienced a rider you become and the more miles you ride, the more you might appreciate a well-fitted touring vehicle.

Quick Tip: Speed is a function of the geometry of the bicycle frame and fork. Although a well-trained cyclist is able to ride faster than a novice, given the same bicycle.

RACING BICYCLES ARE FASTER BECAUSE...

The difference between a mountain, hybrid, or touring bike geometry, and a racing bike geometry may be described as:

The longer the distance between the wheels, the lower the center of gravity of the bicycle, and the more stable the ride. It then stands to reason that, **short wheel-based bicycles with a higher center of gravity, will accelerate and wind-up faster from the start line.** Racing bikes are fun but can be unstable, especially downhill, and have much quicker steering characteristics, especially on corners.

Racing bicycles do not accommodate rear racks, panniers, or other touring accessories because of their short wheelbases. Unless you choose to take your own on tour, there are virtually no companies that offer racing bicycles for their guests. HUBauB

SHOPPING FOR A NEW BIKE

I Want... I Need...I Gotta' Have... A New Bike!!!!

So, you've been making the rounds of bike shops looking for a new bike and are MORE CONFUSED than when you started! You've outgrown your current bike for any of a number of reasons, not the least of which is that everyone else is passing you and you are sick of it! And, somehow all the bikes that you are being shown are starting to look alike.

First off, bicycles from almost every production bike manufacturer (i.e. Cannondale, Trek, Specialized, Schwinn, etc.) and within a certain price range (say $300-$600) ARE a lot alike. We could paint them all one color, remove the decals, and, frankly, the only difference from one bike to another might be the frame material. The REAL difference in any of these bikes is the DEALER from whom you buy it and his (or her) expertise in assembly and willingness to suggest and make the adjustments, changes, and upgrades that will work for your riding needs.

It is important that you get across to the dealer what it is you are looking for in a new bicycle. You might want to think about the following:

• For a MAJORITY of your riding, will you be on road or off? No one bike will truly ride WELL on both dirt and road surfaces. You will have to sacrifice something to use one bike for all riding applications. This also means you may be compromising the one main purpose for which you are buying a new bike.

• Do you want to sit upright? Or, are you thinking about assuming a more traditional road-bike position?

• Do you have any pre-existing conditions that need to be addressed, i.e. a bad back, carpal tunnel syndrome in your hands, or a knee injury?

• Do you like to go FAST?

• Do you want to be able to go farther than you are riding now?

• Will you ever enter a competitive event with this bicycle? Perhaps a biathlon or a citizen's race? By the way, plenty of people use a mountain bike for these events!

• How long do you want this bicycle to last? (This is a trick question - thinking this will be your last bike and loving riding are mutually exclusive)

Be careful of the tendency to think that you will get a bicycle now that is just a little better than the one you already have. First, you will probably outgrow it much more quickly than you think you will, resulting in an additional, unexpected expenditure. And secondly, in today's market, there is a rather large gap in product offering between entry level and really good quality. A truly good bike that you will love every time you ride it, should last five to ten years! When amortized over this period of time, you get a lot for your money when you buy the right bicycle the first time!

NEXT STEPS TO MY NEW BIKE!

First, make a list of all the things that are important to you in a new bike. Absolutely include color if it makes a difference! Also consider those things you do not like about the bike you are riding now. Let's take a sample list from the

"We've Been There" perspective:

Unlike your current bike, you might want a new machine that is:

- lighter
- faster
- will help you climb hills easier
- will be more comfortable and will allow you to ride a lot longer
- shifts better
- stops better
- has equipment for a rack and extra water bottles
- allows you to enter a competitive event now and then

The next step is to discuss your wish list with your local Professional Bicycle Dealer. You might also have a conversation about what you want with fellow riders; remember however, that you will get as many opinions as people polled.

Try to narrow your first round choices down to three or four and then begin test riding some bicycles. Riding too many bikes at one time will make you cranky and confused. It also helps if you ride different kinds of frames equipped with the same component group. Then, you are able to concentrate on the ride qualities of the bicycle instead of trying to compare the ride and the components at the same time.

FRAMESETS

The frameset is the heart and soul of your bicycle. Regardless of the components that hang on it, how your bike rides is more a function of the frame and fork than anything else. The characteristics or ride qualities of your bicycle will depend mostly upon the material, the geometry, and the method by which the tubing is joined into the final frame configuration. Here are some things to think about when looking for a new bike:

How comfortable the frame feels: This is a very personal choice. Frame materials will feel different when riding from one person to the next. However, even a novice rider is able to distinguish the tubing characteristic differences of steel, aluminum, carbon fiber, and titanium, the four materials most often used for framebuilding. You may not know WHAT the differences are; you will however, know what you do and don't like, and that's what counts.

• **Steel is the most traditional of tubing choices.** Steel tubing produces a lively ride, if you have owned a multi-speed bike for many years, steel is probably the type of tubing from which your current bike is constructed. Much has been accomplished in steel tubing technology over the last couple of decades resulting in lighter, stronger, stiffer, and better riding framesets. There are a number of types and grades of steel tubing and several ways in which to produce a steel frame that will change its ride characteristics. (Racers like to say that "steel is real.") Steel frames are either brazed or TIG welded in construction; both work well! Steel frames, when built appropriately, will serve very well for lightweight riders as well as those upwards of 200 pounds and more.

• **Aluminum tubing is lightweight and has the distinct characteristic of dampening the vibrations and shock that are a normal part of riding.** Put another way, it tends to "smooth out" the ride. Aluminum also loses some of the "liveliness" of steel because of this feature. One of the ways in which to identify an aluminum bicycle is that the tubing is often "oversized." Bigger tubes are sometimes necessary to achieve the same tensile strength as steel. To some, this is aesthetically unpleasant; but, "fat" tubes may be worth overlooking if you like the ride quality! Aluminum frames are either TIG welded or may be "bonded" - that is, the joints where the tubes come together are glued and then heated up to make the bond secure. While both methods produce a good quality frame, the end result is a different feel while riding. Our opinion is that a rider over 180 pounds is better served with welding rather than bonding. A TIG welded frame might feel stiffer to ride but will not lose any performance qualities to flexing of the frame.

• **Carbon fiber is very light and strong while exhibiting even more shock absorbing capabilities than aluminum.** We consider carbon fiber a technologically advanced material. When first introduced to the market, it was targeted at competitive riders. Now, however, some builders are beginning to see the tremendous overall benefits for sport and touring applications. Carbon fiber technology has long been used in ships and planes as well as golf clubs and tennis racquets. Methods of construction are by bonding, using aluminum joints to hold the tubes in place; or, the fibers may be "laid up" in a mold which produces a "monocoque" or one-piece construction. We prefer the latter for both strength and performance. We recommend carbon fiber frames for those under 200 pounds.

• **Finally, titanium incorporates all of the best ride characteristics of the other tubing options.** It is also the most expensive frame tubing available. Titanium alloy tubing comes out of the aerospace industry and is "graded" according to aerospace standards. Uncertified titanium may be brittle or unreliable, so we recommend only the most reputable builders for these frames. Titanium must be welded in a special environment with much care and expertise. The tubing offers the added bonus of not having to be painted since it doesn't rust! We have found no rider weight limitations with titanium, depending upon the grade of tubing chosen. Titanium framesets may be the one exception to the "this won't be your last bike" rule.

Quick Tip: Some of what makes a frame ride in a specific and often more desirable way, is the fork that is used on it. We frequently recommend using a carbon fiber fork even though the main frame will be steel, aluminum, or titanium. The carbon acts as an extra shock absorber and offers a very stable downhill ride.

How well the bike climbs and descends is primarily a function of the geometry of the frame, the range of gears, or a combination of both. New technology in suspension stems and front forks can also aid in climbing as well as performing their first intended function - dampening road shock. A quick-climbing race frame has a short wheel base and a strong rear triangle that tucks the rear wheel up under the seat. This is not necessarily a good long distance bike and certainly will not allow the use of rear racks and panniers for extended touring. It is FAST however! This frame will also descend quickly and must be carefully reigned in so as not to attain speeds you are unable to control.

A comfortable touring or "sport" geometry frame that has a longer wheel base will be more stable, especially on the descents. The climbing capabilities will come from the choice a wider range of gearing (see below,) coupled with a well built frameset. The speed at which you climb might be slower, but the comfort is a worthwhile tradeoff. And, you can carry all kinds of stuff on a rack behind you.

How easy it is to get comfortable on the bike may just be the most important area of consideration. If you are constantly trying to find a comfortable position for your hands, rear end, and feet, or find you are not able to breathe freely and easily, something in your position and fit on the bicycle is not right.

Occasionally, no amount of fidgeting with adjustments in saddle, handlebar, or stem positions achieve the desired fit for comfort and efficiency. If this is the case, the frame geometry may just not be appropriate for your body build. Depending upon how much you are willing to put up with and how serious you are about getting the right bicycle, a custom frame might be in order. (We find that

extremely small - under 5' - and tall - over 6'3" - riders tend to be the ones unable to find a stock bicycle that fits well.)

PIECES PARTS

While frame technology evolves more slowly, new component groups, those parts on the bike that make the gears change, the brakes stop, and the wheels turn, seem to be developing yearly. These new groups, in turn, will be what (hopefully) makes a consumer want something new from season to season.

The principal manufacturers of bicycle component groups are Shimano, a Japanese company, Campagnolo, an Italian company, and to a lesser degree, Sachs, from Germany, and Gripshift, from the U.S. There are other, smaller component makers, but these are the most widely used and best known. (In case you are a fisherman, Shimano is the same company that makes reels.)

In the past, Campagnolo was known as "the racing" equipment manufacturer. Today, Campy (as it is affectionately called,) and Shimano are both considered race-worthy component companies. Each offers sport and touring component groups as well, although here Shimano is dominant.

A complete component group usually consists of: brakes, shifters, crank, front and rear derailleurs, chain and cassette (the gear cluster that goes on the rear wheel,) headset (the parts that hold the fork onto the frame,) and occasionally the seat pillar.

An important thing to know about today's gearing systems is that they are, for the most part, proprietary. This means that you cannot mix one company's crank with the other company's chain, shifters, or other essential parts. So, when you talk with the bicycle dealers, they may refer to a

component package as a "gruppo" - (the Italian term for component package!)

Gearing systems on road bikes, or the parts of the bike that make it easier or harder to pedal, are often referred to as "doubles" or "triples," and are what will determine whether you are looking at a racing bike or a sport/touring model. Hybrids and mountain bikes almost always use a triple chainring system, which provides a lot of low or hill climbing gears.

Traditionally, a bicycle with a triple chainring crank immediately implied that is was strictly a touring model. Today, there are new "racing triples" from both Campagnolo and Shimano that offer a wider range of gears than a double crank but still not as low as an all out, cross-country type touring bike.

When you take the number of teeth on the chainrings of the crank in combination with the number of teeth on the cassette that is attached to your rear wheel, you get the "ratio" that some people refer to when talking about the highs and lows of riding. The higher the gear the harder it is to pedal; the lower the gear the easier it is to pedal. **Our theory on changing gears is simple: when it gets too hard to pedal, shift to an easier gear!** Do you need to know which one? Not really - if you want to learn all of that, you will.

Quick Tip: The term "granny gear" refers to an extremely low gear ratio - often 1:1 - that allows you to climb straight up a tree... well, just about any incline! Unless you are traveling with full packs through REAL mountains, this gear ratio is rarely needed!

BOTTOM LINE ?

We've talked about tubing, components, ride qualities, and frame geometry. Still, when you walk in to the bike shop, you will be confronted with a myriad of brands and models, depending upon what that particular dealer is selling. YOU still have to make the final choice. Here are some things to keep in mind:

• When looking at production bicycles, the manufacturer has already chosen the geometry of the frame and the component group.

• Most companies offer quite a few stock frame sizes and, with careful attention to saddle, bar, and stem sizes and adjustments, there are not too many people who will fall outside of a standard size.

• Component packages are selected for particular reasons including meeting a specific price point and performance level.

• The higher the price, the better the quality, especially for the components. (Some manufacturers use the same frameset for all bicycles in a certain category and specify higher quality component packages as their prices go up.)

WHAT ABOUT A CUSTOM FRAME?

If you have decided to go beyond what is offered from production bike manufacturers, we highly recommend looking at frames built in the United States. After more than twenty years in the bicycle business, we have found that today's American framebuilders are some of the best in the world.

There is sometimes the nostalgic reason of "tradition" for buying Italian, French, or British, but, we would disagree that these frames are better quality than an American one of the same tubing and construction type. And, especially where new technology is concerned, more research and development is being done in the U.S. than anywhere else in the world.

While there are ordinarily quite a few choices from a custom house, even in "stock" frames, the biggest advantage of a hand built frame is that it will be to your specifications; i.e. size, color, tubing, geometry, etc. In addition, you can choose the component package you want and need to fit your riding style and capabilities. Custom bikes take a lot of planning and are expensive. Very often, your frame will not be made until you order it and delivery can take as long as two or three months. Is it worth it? Talk with cyclists who own bikes like these and, by all means RIDE SOME!

Finally, it is important to take the time to really try different bikes. Whether you understand the technical and mechanical advantages of one bike over another is irrelevant. What is important is that you get a bike that has been assembled properly, fits you well, and with which you are both comfortable and happy. As always, we are here to help talk you through any questions or problems you might have.

TIRES AND TUBES
"Flat Tires Are A Drag!"

Flat tires are a drag! And, not knowing what kind or size tire and tube you need or how much air you should put into your tires is even more of a drag. The subject is often confusing, so we'll try to keep it as simple as possible.

Quick Tip: The easiest way to know what size tire you need is to LOOK ON THE SIDEWALL OF THE TIRE YOU ALREADY HAVE! The size will be visible and may read something like 700 x 25 or 26 x 1.75.

Let's begin with the various types of tires. Road bikes and most hybrids use what is commonly termed a "700C" tire. The 700 refers to the circumference (although it doesn't REALLY measure 700 anything) and the C refers to centimeters. Once you have determined that you need a 700C tire, you need to know what WIDTH 700C tire you want or need. Tire width has a direct relationship to the wheel's rim size, so NOT ALL 700C TIRES FIT ALL 700C RIMS.

The easy solution is to once again look at the sidewall to see what was already on the wheel and duplicate that tire size. However, there is some flexibility in what you are ABLE to use on the wheel and, this flexibility will change the characteristics of the ride. Here's how it goes:

The wider the tire, the more cushioned, the more stable, and the slower the ride. The narrower the tire, the less resistance you will feel from the road surface

resulting in a faster but harsher ride. Another way to look at it might be in the "performance " of the bike terms of acceleration and speed. A narrow, very high pressure tire will accelerate and roll faster. It will also transfer more of the road shock to you and create a less stable ride. Trade-offs!

Here is a very common scenario: A new rider will start off with the most stable tire/wheel combination he or she can find. As the rider becomes more familiar with the bike and more confident while cycling he/she will one day come to the realization that other riders are whizzing by while he/she is working VERY HARD and falling further and further behind.

The next scene finds our tired and frustrated rider back at the bike shop looking for ways to go faster with less effort. And, the first suggestion is almost always a narrower, higher pressure tire. Make certain that if this is a choice you are thinking of making, the rim on your bicycle is compatible with the new tire you are choosing. A rim that is too wide for the tire may allow the tire to blow off after it is inflated. BANG!

Quick tip: It is very important to remember that your tires are like shock absorbers. Careful attention should always be paid to proper inflation- which, in our opinion, is the maximum called for when riding on the road.

27" or 700C...Sew up or Clincher...what DOES it all mean?

27" wheels are becoming obsolete. Up until a few years ago, only high performance racing bicycles were offered with 700C wheels. Today, virtually every bicycle maker has chosen the 700C size-for their hybrids and road bikes - offering the market a fairly universal tire (yay!).

Since this is the case, if you still have a bicycle with 27" rims on it, be aware that there are only a few tire manufacturers left who offer any choices in 27" tires. You would have to have wheels built to accommodate 700C tires if you wanted to change them and there is a good probability that your brake shoes would not reach the rims if you decided to buy new wheels. (Sounds like a new bike to me!).

Most importantly, a 700C tire will NOT fit a 27" wheel rim. Don't even try it! The experience will be both fruitless and frustrating! The 700C tire is slightly smaller than the 27" rim and, no matter how much prodding and prying you apply, well, you get the picture.

<u>Most **mountain** bikes have 26" tires.</u> We wish we knew why these tires use an "inch" designation while the road and hybrid tires use centimeters-but, we don't. What we do know is that all of what we said holds true for 26" tires. The sizes are still printed on the sidewalls and narrow or wide choices are available depending upon your rim size.

One extra factor to take into consideration might be the tread of a mountain bike tire. An aggressive, knobby tire will bite down into the dirt and mud, offering a tremendous amount of traction and stability. Of course, the trade off is on-the-road performance in the forms of speed and acceleration. There are quite a few types of smooth tires available for mountain rims, just make certain that the ones you choose are compatible with the rims you have.

If you have a bicycle with 26" tires and it is a traditional 10-speed style road bike, it is probably a domestically produced, mass-marketed bicycle such as Huffy or Murray. These bicycles are not ordinarily as suitable for serious adult riding because they offer no choices in frame sizes and seem to have recurring mechanical problems, especially with broken spokes and bent rims. The tire size for these bicycles is almost always 26 x 1 3/8".

Finally <u>**there are two types of rims - clincher and sew-up (sometimes referred to as tubular)**</u>. 98+% of all bicycles produced for sale in this country use clincher tires on clincher rims. This means that there is an inner tube inside the tire that may be removed, patched and/or easily replaced.

Sew-up (or tubular) tires, on the other hand, are glued to the rim and are used by riders who are either looking for ULTIMATE performance or who are racing. These tires are expensive, and, when a rider gets a flat tire, there is no way to fix the puncture. The tube is actually SEWN into the tire casing-hence the name sew-up! If you have sew-up wheels, remember to let the glue dry for 24 hours before riding.

LET'S TALK ABOUT INNER TUBES

Okay, here is what an inner tube does - IT HOLDS AIR! If you take an inner tube out of a box and just keep blowing it up it becomes enormous and all out of shape. The tire is what gives the tube its shape and the tube is what gives the

tire its shock absorbing capabilities – nice symbiosis, huh?

You need to know a little more though. There are two types of valves on inner tubes – PRESTA and SCHRAEDER *(see diagrams)*. While the tire does NOT care which type of valve is on the tube, your rim and your pump do.

PRESTA VALVES are high pressure and need to be opened before air can be pumped in. After filling your tires, they need to be closed so that air doesn't leak out with each turn of the wheel when the bicycle is in motion. (Some people refer to presta valves as European valves.)

SCHRAEDER VALVES are just like the ones on your car. The air may be pumped into the valve without opening or closing it.

So, why do you want to go to the trouble of using a presta valve? The simple (and smart aleck) answer is because the manufacturer used a presta drilled rim on your bicycle. Not buying that answer? Okay,

The technical answer is BECAUSE IT OFFERS YOU HIGHER PRESSURE CAPABILITIES. Take a look at the sidewall of your tire again. This time, you are looking for a PSI or "pounds per square inch" rating. Many of the road tires require pressures in excess of 100psi and Schraeder valves are not as reliable at these pressures.

It is important to keep your tires inflated to maximum pressure while riding on the road for several reasons:

• Your tires are your shock absorbers. Maximum pressure will help you prevent all that road shock from traveling up the forks through your handlebars, and into your hands, arms and shoulders.

• Maximum pressure will help protect your rim if you should happen to hit something.

• Full pressure will help prevent pinch flats from both the weight of your body on the bike and again if you happen to hit something.

Finally, carry an extra tube or two with you at all times. More than once or twice we have seen riders get into a situation where both tires go flat and one tube doesn't help. The extra $3.00 or $4.00 isn't worth a 5 or 10 mile walk home!

PRESTA VALVE
(NOT like your car tire)

SCHRAEDER VALVE
(like your car tire)

Quick Tip:
You cannot get air into a presta valve with a Schraeder pump head and vice versa.

Now you know about the two types of inner tube valves; more importantly, you need to know that inflation devices, whether pumps, CO2 cartridges, or the hose on the compressor at the gas station, also need to match the type of valve on your inner tube – presta or Schraeder – or NO AIR!

Most pumps purchased from a bicycle shop can be easily converted to either type of valve stem. The directions are usually graphically described on the package. This way, you are carrying the type of pump you need.

In addition there is a small adapter that will screw onto a presta valve to convert it to a Schraeder so that you can use almost any inflation device that is intended for bicycles, cars, and other inflatable products. These little adapters are made of either brass or aluminum, cost under $1.00. We recommend buying two – they're small!

You must remember to open the presta valve, screw the adapter onto it and pump up the tube – either a regular bicycle pump, a gas station compressor hose, or an instant inflation device. Remember to remove the adapter and close the valve when you have reached the desired pressure. You can then re-screw the adapter onto the valve stem and leave it there until you need it the next time. It doesn't weigh much and you won't wonder where it is if you need it!

Finally, keep an eye on the condition of your tires and tubes. Good quality bicycle tires can last upwards of 2,5000 miles. Pay particular attention to cuts in either the tread or sidewalls and watch out for glass and other sharp objects on the ground. We also find that in areas where there is a lot of air polution the tires seem to be affected and will not last as long.

SIZE AND FIT
Whaddya' Mean
By That?

When the touring company asks what size bicycle you want, they may also give you guidelines as to how to go about determining your size. If this is a new frontier for you, check with a reputable Professional Bicycle Dealer or measure your own bicycle. (Do this only if you find you are usually comfortable riding your bicycle for extended periods of time. If you do not find your own bike easy and fun to ride, why not? Take it to your friendly PBD and get re-fitted on it. ASAP!)

Quick Tip: Bicycles are measured by frame size, not wheel size.

Frame size is ordinarily defined one of two ways: center-to-center of the top tube or center-to-top of the top tube. The variance may be as much as ¾"-1" overall, so it does make a difference. Center of the crank (see the diagram) to center of the top tube (A) or, center of the crank to the top of the top tube (B), may be measured

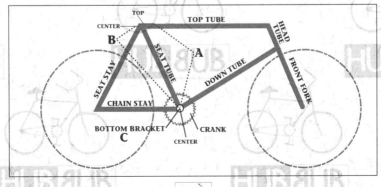

in inches or centimeters. If the bicycle has a sloping top tube (or is a lady's frame,) the measurement is using an "imaginary" top tube that is parallel to the floor.

If you think you ride a 27" bicycle - beware - you would have to have an inseam of almost 38" to comfortably ride this machine - that would mean you were nearly 7' tall! The terms 27" or 26" refer to the bicycle WHEEL measurement, not frame size!

To determine the correct frame size for you, add between 10 " and 11" to the height of the bicycle off the floor at the bottom bracket (C). The total should be equal to or just shy of your inseam length or, crotch-to-floor measurement in bare feet. Example: A 22" frame + 11"off the floor = 33" inseam or a 56cm frame + 27.97cm off the floor = 83.94cm inseam. (Still a 33" inseam!!)

Rule-of-thumb states that: there should be about 1" to 1 1/2 " of space between you and the top tube of a touring bike; between 1 1/2 " to 2" on a hybrid, and as much as 4" to 5" of stand-over room on a mountain bike.

When given the frame sizes available by your tour director, choose the CLOSEST to this formula as you can. If you must compromise, err toward the smaller frame for added safety in mounting and dismounting.

Bear in mind that the smaller the frame, the more you will have to lean over to reach the handlebars. And, while being able to stand over the top tube is important to your safety in mounting and dismounting - it is not the only important criterion for fit.... your ability to comfortably reach the handlebars and BRAKE LEVERS is equally important.

Which brings us to a very important technical aspect that we need to emphasize. *Handlebar stems can only be raised a fraction of the amount that a seat pillar can.* There is a "limit line" etched into the handlebar stem. If you raise the handlebar stem beyond that line, you are in danger of having it break off, resulting in a nasty accident!

Stiff and sore neck, shoulders, and hands, fingers that fall asleep while riding, and lower back pains are all conditions that would point to a stem that is too low. The correct solution is replacing it with one that has a longer "quill" - the part that goes down in to the fork. THIS IS NOT A "DO-IT-YOURSELF-AT-HOME-JOB" FOR MOST PEOPLE! It requires removing all the stuff on at least one side of your handlebars, including brake levers, shifters, cables, and tape, and reinstalling and adjusting everything after the new stem is in place.

Having said all that, sitting too upright, especially for longer distances, has its own drawbacks. You become the windshield, which creates a lot of fatigue, and you may actually put a considerable amount of pressure on your hips and tailbone. There is a proper balance and it is a process to find it. Don't give up, it is worth the effort!

For ladies who wish to ride a women's or step-through frame, the most important factors will be hand/arm/seat comfort and forward reach when on the saddle. Standover is not important - there is no top tube to contend with!

GETTING COMFORTABLE ON YOUR BICYCLE IS A PROCESS.

Final adjustments after the correct bicycle has been chosen can be made by the tour directors on site at the beginning of the ride. If you have measurements from a bicycle you have been riding at home, by all means, WRITE THEM DOWN - BRING THEM ALONG - and try to duplicate the configuration with your tour bike. Raising or lowering saddles, moving them fore and aft, tilting handlebars a little forward or backward are all easy, one wrench adjustments and will add immeasurably to a pleasant experience.

Your overall position on the bicycle while you are pedaling is the most important factor to comfort and fit. There are dozens and dozens of articles on how to achieve correct position and fit. There are ideals and there are ideas. Remember that getting comfortable on your bicycle is a process. Be willing to go through it. Make small, incremental changes and keep track of them. Measure everything before you begin and write it down. This could be considered the "blueprint" of your bicycle.

Want more advice on bicycles and fit ? For starters, locate your PBD - the best in the area. If you need help finding one or just want to bounce some ideas off of us, call, write, fax, or email us.

We realize we haven't mentioned that unmentionable - YOUR DERRIERE - BIG topic (just kidding!) Next chapter please! HUBBUB

• Saddles • What To Wear • Cycling Amenities • Helmets • Pedals & Shoes • What To Take •

SADDLES -
or Oh! My Aching Derrier...

Quick Tip: It's shape and support, not width and cushion that count!

HONEST.... Just because a saddle feels like a down pillow and belongs on a John Deere tractor does not mean it is a suitable platform upon which you should perch your delicate derriere and ride 35-50 miles per day for a week. In fact, more damage has been done to not only buttocks, but hips, knees, genitals, and feet because of the wrong saddle and saddle positioning.

Every year, the market sees a plethora of new saddles from which to choose. Research is ongoing to find better shapes, materials, and coverings.

There are saddles for women and saddles for men. There are racing saddles, touring saddles, mountain bike saddles, and exercise saddles, each offering a variety of shapes, coverings, cushions, and undercarriages. Research is perennially and persistently ongoing in an effort to find the "perfect" saddle for all derrieres. Our guess is, so long as people are different, derrieres will be different, and we will continue to need a variety of saddles!

Saddle shapes are chosen by manufacturers based upon such criteria as width of hips, how forward or back one should sit on a specific saddle, or any of a number of other possible "ideas," some more random than others.

Different types of coverings include leather, lycra, and other newly developed synthetic materials. Leather breathes, you can easily slide forward and back on lycra, and some of the newer synthetics can achieve both. Cushioning may be in the form of foam, gel, or a combination of the two. Some saddles have no cushioning whatsoever! (There's a name for people who can ride "hard" saddles!)

There is also new technology that has produced built-in, under-carriage "shock absorbers" and spring systems. Manufacturers are also experimenting with special designs that reduce upward pressure by cutting away very specific areas of the base, as well as with cutaways in the tailbone section on the top of the saddle.

Our first advice is, try some of the adjustments we talk about further along in this chapter. If you decide you need a new saddle, try to "test ride" some. See if your favorite bicycle shop has a "happy tushy" guarantee and will give you a 20 or 30 mile test ride allowance. Perhaps you can try one or two out in the shop on a trainer and at least eliminate the absolutely worst candidates.

If you have made all the adjustments and tried a series of saddles but are still experiencing problems, we might suggest a gel-filled saddle pad. It can be quickly installed over your existing saddle, and with just a cinch of the drawstring, you can add an instant shock-absorbing liquid gel - "ahhhhhhhh" to your ride. These saddle pads are portable and inexpensive. They can also be heavy and will add height to your existing saddle so you may need to lower your seat pillar. (Measure your present seat height before installing a pad!)

SO, WHAT IS THE RIGHT PLACE FOR MY SEAT?

When attempting to find solutions to persistent saddle

problems, the questions we always ask include:

- Is your pain more forward or rearward?
- Do your "sit" bones hurt?
- Do you have any chafing or "rawness?" This includes sores, rashes, or boils.
- Are you experiencing any genital numbness? (STOP RIDING IMMEDIATELY IF THIS IS THE CASE!)
- Have you ridden enough miles to get yourself a little "broken in?"
- Are you sitting squarely on the saddle?
- Do you push yourself off the back of the saddle or slide forward while riding?

All of these things are important to your comfort; and, especially to your ability to ride extended mileage day-after-day. Raising or lowering, tilting the nose up or down, or sliding your saddle back and forth on its rails just a tiny

fraction may make all the difference in the way you feel. Remember that you must be comfortable WHILE RIDING, so if you make adjustments while in a stationary trainer, it may not accurately reflect how you will feel while out on the road.

Do not attempt to make several changes all at once. This usually results in not knowing what helped and what didn't. Try one small change at a time and give it some miles. If you can determine immediately that a change doesn't work, go back to your starting point.

When you have made an adjustment, write it down. Use a piece of masking tape on your seat pillar as a mark for seat height. That way, you always know where you began. Measure the distance from the nose of your saddle to the center of the handlebar stem bolt and write it down. This measurement lets you know where your seat is positioned fore and aft.

The correct pedaling

motion is a circle. Achieving the correct position on your bicycle will be the means by which you can accomplish the correct motion, get the most power out of your pedal stroke, and be most comfortable while doing it. There are three critical saddle adjustments: height, fore and aft position, and tilt.

Saddle tilt is the easiest to figure out. If the nose is up to high, guess where it's poking you? If the nose is too low, you will be sliding off the front of the saddle. Begin at level and work from there. Many people find that a slight upward tilt is the most comfortable.

Saddle height is the most controversial. There are a bazillion articles about this subject and none took YOU into consideration! We can only give you the following guidelines:

• A saddle that is positioned too high over-extends your legs, allows your hips to rock, and will probably make your knees hurt on one side or the other (or both.)

• A saddle that is positioned too low under-extends your legs, robs you of maximum pedaling power, and will probably make your knees hurt under or near the kneecap.

• A saddle that is positioned appropriately may mean that you CANNOT reach the ground with your toes or feet while sitting and pedaling. (You never ride while standing on the ground - trust us on this one!)

• If you are afraid of not being able to touch the ground, you need to spend time learning to mount and dismount your bicycle until you are able to be confident in doing so. Try this:

• To mount: stand over the top tube of your bike, put one foot on a pedal, and boost yourself up onto the saddle while pushing off forward with the other foot. Pedal.

• To dismount: begin to come to a stop, stand onto one pedal and step down

with the other foot.

• *Height Adjustments*

• While sitting on the bike, with the balls of your feet positioned over the axles of the pedals, drop your foot to the straight up and down (6:00) position.

• If all is well, you should have a slight bend in your needs.

• Now, drop your heel as far down as it will go.

• If all is well, you should be at maximum extension.

Fore and aft positioning needs to take a whole lot of other factors into consideration. If you are not positioned over the crank appropriately, you cannot possibly turn that circle with your pedals - you will be turning some version of an ellipse. Especially if you find you have pushed your saddle all the way forward or all the way back on your seat rails, a variety of things can happen that will affect your pedaling power and efficiency. An unbalanced fore and aft position may also indicate that your

bicycle's top tube or handlebar stem extension is too long or too short for you.

• *Scenario #1:*
You've pushed your saddle all the way forward to comfortably reach the handlebars and brake levers. The probable cause is that the top tube length, the handlebar stem extension, or a combination of both are too long - the results may be:

• you are too far over the crank, creating a choppy, "pistoning" pedal motion. Not good for your knees and inefficient.

• you are too far over the front end of the bike, creating an uneven distribution of weight. This can, in turn, allow the rear end of the bike to come up off the ground unexpectedly. You could lose control and fall.

• *Scenario #2:*
You've moved your

saddle all the way back on the rails because you feel too scrunched up and can't breathe correctly - the top tube length, your handlebar stem extension, or a combination of both are too short - the results may be:

• you are too far behind the crank, creating a "paddling" pedal motion. This is not good for your hips and will rob you of that all important power.

• you are putting too much weight on your hips and tailbone.

• you may not have enough weight on the front of the bike, allowing the front wheel to come off the ground unexpectedly. You could lose control and fall.

• an added unwanted result of this combination is there is no seat rail left to add a seat pack!

• *Scenario #3:*

Your saddle is positioned right where it belongs! Everything is peachy!

Fore and aft results:

• While sitting on the bike, with the balls of your feet positioned over the axles of the pedals, move your right foot at the 3:00 position (see diagram).

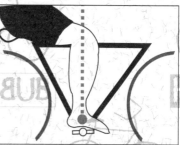

• If all is well, you will be able to "drop an imaginary plumb line" through your knee and it should line up with or be slightly behind (+/- 1cm) the ball of your foot.

As an added note: there is ALWAYS some latitude in these recommended adjustments. There is no one quite like you. Never take what one person says about size and fit as gospel! Remember that it is a

6

process, it takes time, and the results are worth it!

Also remember that even with proper positioning and a new saddle or saddle pad, all your discomfort might not go away. Padded cycling shorts without intrusive seams (and this means NO TRADITIONAL UNDERWEAR OR JEANS while riding!) and diligent use of a medicated chamois cream will help to avoid things like saddle sores, blisters, chafing, and boils.

You need to take good care of your derriere during your trip or you will be riding in the SAG wagon instead of on your bike! In the end (of course that pun was intended!) TAKE YOUR PERSONAL SADDLE OR SADDLE PAD ON TOUR WITH YOU! The tour director will be more than happy to install your saddle on your rental bike.

Finally, if you are unable to achieve a position that feels right, given all the adjustments available to you, begin looking into the specific geometry of the bicycle and the idiosyncrasies of your build. For instance, men traditionally have long torsos and shorts legs - women just the opposite. If you know, for example that you have very short arms, you may need a very short handlebar stem extension, even though you need a relatively tall bike. DO NOT DEPEND UPON WHAT THE MANUFACTURER HAS DECIDED is right for you. Work with a reputable shop to make YOUR BIKE FIT COMFORTABLY TO YOUR SPECIFICATIONS. HUB&UB

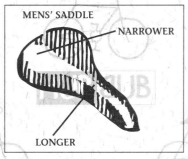

MENS' SADDLE

NARROWER

LONGER

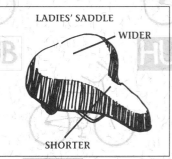

LADIES' SADDLE

WIDER

SHORTER

WHAT TO WEAR
After All, It's Not WHO You Are That Counts!

The adage that "clothing makes the man" (and woman, of course) takes on a whole new meaning when it comes to cycling. Having just enough to wear and of the right stuff will make your cycling adventure a lot more enjoyable!

One of the terms frequently used when referring to the "right stuff" is "layering." The term sort of speaks for itself. The reasons for layering your activewear however, are twofold: first, because you will choose garments that are lighter weight, layers allow you more freedom of movement; second, layering gives you the option of taking off or putting on a garment as the day progresses without changing your entire outfit.

Most of the apparel and products we recommend have technical origins. Either the fabrics offer some sort of moisture management system, such as wicking dampness away from the skin, or afford some sort of protection from wind, sun, or rain. Choosing several technically appropriate, lightweight layers will add to your flexibility and comfort instead of allowing you to become wet, cold, uncomfortable and overdressed like the "Michelin© Man."

Knowing what-to-wear-when is a process, much like the process of fitting your bicycle until it feels comfortable for longer mileage. We can explain what each type of garment does and how it was intended to be used, but we cannot determine how cold, warm, wet, or dry you will be under any particular circumstances. You will have to try various combinations and see how they fare for you.

Please read our **Fabric Primer** for more technical information about the textiles involved. And, as always, if a question is not answered to your satisfaction here, please call, write, email, or fax us.

Here we go.........

Quick Tip:- Technical apparel works!

There are fabrics that pull moisture away from your skin (we'll use the term wicking,) and fabrics that stop moisture from building up inside a garment, (we'll call these breathable.) There is specially designed padding for shorts and undergarments, lightweight insulators for cool days, and well-ventilated outerwear for rain and cold. Each has been

developed to keep you comfortable depending upon the climatic conditions.

You will especially value the garments that provide easy solutions to abrupt temperature changes. You will find them indispensable when you get up in the morning and it is 38° only to get on the road and have the temperature rise to 75° a few hours later; and, your luggage is already at the next B&B awaiting your arrival.

You will appreciate being able to rinse out a lightweight, seamless undergarment and find it dry within an hour, particularly when your regular cycling shorts would still be soaking wet the next morning because you didn't remember to wash them until midnight!

All of the technical fabrics that we recommend have been tested by cyclists! We know that they work and do exactly what they were intended to do. In choosing garments and fabrics for your specific purposes, here

are a few areas
for consideration:

- What time of year will you be traveling?
- How long will you be on tour?
- What are the customs of the country (countries) to which you are traveling?
- Are rain and/or wind normal conditions of the area in which you will be traveling?
- Are wide temperature swings to be expected?
- Do you tend to get cold or hot easily?
- Do you tend to perspire a great deal? (If you do not perspire at all, that is a potentially dangerous problem!)
- Are your hands prone to any stiffness or numbness?

As always, if anything raises a question for you that is not answered... call, fax, phone, email... you've got the routine down by now!

APPAREL BASICS.- #1 - BOTTOMS

Shorts

....

Quick-Tip: Padded cycling shorts are the best for any and all extended riding.

....

That was easy to say. However, be prepared to do some research and "on the bike testing" to find the right cycling shorts for you. We can make specific recommendations, but truth be told, not every manufacturer's shorts work for every bottom.

Cycling shorts are available for both men and women, although some companies only offer a "unisex" product. The cuts can be very different so a non-gender specific short may not work for you.

Regardless of gender, cycling shorts offer four very specific advantages: 1.) strategically placed padding, 2.) absence of seams, 3.) multiple-panel construction, and 4.) long-leg length.

There are probably a few other less significant reasons to use a cycling short (how about, looking cool?) but these are REALLY important.

PADDING: The padded crotch section, frequently called a chamois (the original European cycling shorts used real chamois leather,) may be made of polypropylene - a hydrophobic (water-hating) filament usually spun into a quick-drying, terrycloth-like fabric - or a synthetic suede-like material, or a combination of the two. Some sort of closed-cell foam is usually sewn under the next-to-skin piece for extra cushioning. There are also shorts that use a liquid gel "bladder" sewn into the crotch. This bladder is then covered with a wicking fabric. The gel offers a kind of shock absorption although some riders find these shorts bulky and hot. This is strictly personal preference and those who use a gel short - LOVE 'EM!

Padding for women may also contain a cotton center strip for hygienic reasons.

Several European manufacturers are using chamois-sections that have been treated with an anti-bacterial substance in an attempt to keep any kind of infection from arising. (More on this subject elsewhere!)

ABSENCE OF SEAMS: In our saddle section, we mentioned that you should NOT wear traditional underwear with cycling shorts. There are two reasons that make underwear undesirable for cycling: 1.) the elastic sewn into the leg holes of the underwear can "dig in" around your upper leg and 2.) SEAMS - ouch-ouch-ouch-ouch-ouch! Seams can literally "cut" you while sitting on a saddle and pedaling for any length of time. Some manufacturers have found a way to keep the chamois area 100% free of any type of seams (one-piece construction) while others stitch the padded crotch into the short so that seams are not in places that will irritate you.

Quick-Tip: One person's dream short is another person's nightmare. This is THE MOST PERSONAL of choices. Also, it does NOT follow that the most expensive short will be the best choice for you. The best fit with the appropriate padding will be the best choice!

THE MULTIPLE PANELS of a good cycling short offer a more anatomic fit, especially in the cycling position. There is no fabric-bunching while pedaling and your legs can move freely in all directions. The term "8-panel" construction usually signifies a top-of-the-line product, although some manufacturers are experimenting with fewer and fewer panels in an attempt to streamline the fit even more. Multiple panels are SEWN together - so there are seams. They are not ordinarily in "strategically sensitive" areas however.

THE LONGER LEGS provide fabric further down on your thighs to help prevent any chafing from the pedaling motion of your thighs against the sides of the saddle. The bottom of the leg may have a "soft" elastic band or "grippers" to keep the short from creeping up while riding. These should not be too tight or they will cut off your circulation while riding. The only disadvantage in the longer legs is the weird tan line.

One style of cycling short is called **bib-shorts.** Add an upper body, over-the-shoulders strap system to a standard pair of lycra-type cycling shorts and - voila' - bibs! If you especially find that, no matter what you do, your shorts keep slipping down in the back while you are riding, bibs will solve that problem. So long as the straps are wide, flat, and comfortable without digging in to your shoulders, we think bibs are a terrific idea!

Fabrics from which most classic-style cycling shorts are constructed afford many advantages. These textiles are usually synthetic and offer such properties as moisture management (which is just one more reason to wear your cycling shorts next to the skin!) and UV screening. The fabrics are long lasting, wash cleanly and easily, and feel silky and comfortable. Cotton/lycra™ combinations are available for those who like the feel of natural fibers. They will retain more moisture than the synthetic fabrics and take longer to dry, however.

THE SKIN-TIGHT ALTERNATIVE

If you think the skin-tight lycra™ shorts are too revealing or you just cannot get comfortable with the look (WE, however, do not think you look like a stuffed sausage!) there are some variations on the skin-tight theme. -One is a standard, lycra-based short that has been sewn into a lightweight, fuller-cut nylon or cotton overshort. The quality of the under-short portion is excellent and the lightweight overshort does have the built-in advantage of pockets! There are also some manufacturers who use a "suspended padded brief"

sewn into a nylon or cotton outer short. While this is similar to an underwear-type solution, some people have found these to work well for them.

Quick Tip: Cycling shorts must be washed out daily! (keeps the critters away!)

UNDERGARMENTS FOR DOWN BELOW

Quick-Tip: Cycling-specific underwear is a great way to extend the wear-cycle of your padded cycling shorts while traveling.

Because padded cycling shorts MUST be washed every time they are worn (or beware the consequences... infections, sores, critters, and worse!) there are a couple of splendid alternatives for traveling.

The **unpadded undergarment**, made of a combination of lycra™ and a quick drying synthetic that feels and acts like cotton, is a thin, seamless, unpadded liner that can be very effective when used in conjunction with regular cycling shorts. They mimic the silhouette of a cycling short with longer legs and are usually available in either black or white. Liners take up just a tiny bit of luggage space, readily rinse clean, and dry in a heartbeat! They will also save you having to wash your regular cycling shorts daily. (Although we recommend that you still wash them every other day even if using liners.) Liners may also help to stave off infection by keeping you a little drier.

There are also **padded undergarments** that can be used to turn any non-padded short into a "cycling" short. Still offering a longer legged profile, padded undergarments do not provide nearly the amount or styles of padding available from an authentic cycling short, but they are still waaay better than nothing at all!

Finally, if you think you might favor a "brief-style" undergarment, both padded and unpadded versions are available. Bear in mind, this underwear offers a minimal amount of padding and the added disadvantage of elastic around the top of your thigh.

LEG WARMERS, TIGHTS, AND RAIN/WIND PANTS

One of the more useful and generally underrated products ever to be developed for the cyclist is a pair of **leg warmers.** This is the garment to which we were referring for those cooler mornings followed by warm afternoons. As a simple means of protection from the wind and cold, leg warmers are ordinarily constructed of a spandex-lycra™ based fabric that has been "brushed" on the inside providing a little extra warmth. (We often use the term "roubaix" for this brushed effect.)

Leg warmers cover from thigh to ankle and snug up right under the cuff of your cycling short with a soft band of elastic, which helps them to remain in place. There are zippers at the ankles so you need not remove your shoes to put them on or take them off. When not needed, they roll up small enough to jam into your jersey pocket or seat pack.

Good quality leg warmers also have an "articulated" (hinged or connected) knee area so there is no fabric bunching behind the knee and plenty of freedom of movement. Occasionally, someone with VERY thin legs finds that leg warmers won't stay put - so, on to the next option....tights. (P.S. There are also arm warmers that accomplish the same thing!)

Tights are another topic all together. To say there are a few styles of tights is like saying there are a few brands of bikes! But, for our purposes, tights are usually unpadded, pull on like a pair of pantyhose, have a drawstring waist, and may be zippered at the ankles or have under-the-foot stirrups to keep them from riding up.

There are probably a dozen different fabric weights available from 4 oz. lycra™ (bathing suit material,) through a heavy duty, fully insulated version that has a windproof, waterproof, and breathable front panel, and several fabric types including wool blends. We think that a tight similar to the fabric used for leg warmers is the most versatile, offering a moderate amount of both warmth and wind protection.

Tights with padded-seats are available for those times when you know you will NOT be taking the tights off during a ride. However, most cyclists will use an unpadded tight, often pulling them on over their cycling shorts. There are also bib tights that offer the over-the-shoulder-strap system as well as some extra fabric to help keep your upper body warm.

You will need to think about weather conditions, time of year, etc. in deciding whether to take a pair of tights with you. Regardless of whether you take them on tour, tights are a great item

of clothing to have in your cycling wardrobe for cool weather riding and training. Unpadded tights may also be used for cross-country skiing, walking, and running... making them an excellent investment for the multi-sport athlete.

Rain or Wind Pants are an interesting topic. Again, there are a variety from which to choose depending upon things like how waterproof and breathable they are. These long-legged pants are usually designed to go on over your shorts or tights, have zippers at the bottom, and are fuller cut with "articulated" knees (allowing full pedaling motion.) They are especially useful on trips where you need to ride a set number of miles on a day-to-day basis, regardless of weather, and may find yourself in a day-long drizzle or wind and cold. Very often, rain pants may be part of a 2-piece rain suit.

Best case scenario: Rain only occurs one week prior or one week subsequent to YOUR tour plans! Fat chance...

Quick-Tip for cold/rainy days: Most heat loss occurs through the head, neck, and upper body. Keeping these areas dry, warm, and comfortable will make your trip more enjoyable!

APPAREL BASICS - #2 - TOPS

Quick-Tip: always wear a shirt while riding... nuthin' hurts more than taking a spill, and sliding down the road on your bare skin!!!!

JERSEYS - Uh, oh! it's that stuffed sausage syndrome again... at least most women think that the lycra, racing-style jerseys, while colorful and often printed with fun designs, cut them off right at those hips! So, what is appropriate to wear on top? Frankly, just about anything! with the following caveat.... cotton, once wet, stays wet. Not good!

Dry is the key to comfort for your upper body. Even in the wind, you will probably perspire faster than most cotton based fabrics can dry. Should the temperature drop even a few degrees, you will find a cotton top leaves you wet, cold, and miserable. Because there are probably no zippers in your cotton-based T-shirt, you can't get any ventilation either.

Most "technical" jerseys are made from a polyester-based yarn that has been designed to both wick and breathe. The finished fabric acts like two materials bonded together so that as the inside of the garment wicks moisture toward the outside, the air dries the moisture quickly not allowing the garment to become soaked. For those who perspire like a running faucet, this works pretty well but not 100%. Other technical advances have been made with fabrics that screen ultraviolet rays - often up to 70%.

Ever wonder why there are little pockets sewn onto the back of cycling jerseys?

REAL simple .... FOOD! You can stuff a banana or energy bar into your rear jersey pocket and readily reach back to get it while still on your bike. If you wore arm or leg warmers and find it is time to remove them, you can easily roll them up and stuff them in one of those handy rear pockets. In Europe, cyclists often used their rear pockets for a scrunched up rain jacket or cotton team cap, even a folded up tire or inner tube!

Most jerseys have a front zipper. Some are short, maybe 10-12cm - but some are very long, which facilitates "venting" while on the road - so, ladies, please wear an undergarment you aren't ashamed of showing off when unzipping your jersey to the world!

Finally, the MOST important reason for a cycling jersey - IT MAKES THE OUTFIT!!!!

UNDERGARMENTS FOR UP-TOP

FOR WOMEN.... (no peeking, guys!)

A sport bra is a good thing for most women..The reasons to spend a little extra money on a good sport bra are that they often look okay alone (so you can get that tan!) and most importantly, they give MUCH better support than a regular bra. Support is especially significant for those riding touring bicycles in the "10 speed" or bent over position and for larger breasted women ("D" cup and over.) Sport bras may be worn instead of regular bras for off-riding days, so you need not take extra undergarments unless you wish.

UNISEX ... (come on back now, men)

For cooler weather, there are hydrophobic (water-hating) undergarments, often available in several weights. These "base layers," as we like to refer to them, are made from a polyester-based filament that has been spun into a fabric. The fabric has only one property - it HATES moisture and will wick wetness away from your skin and transfer it to the outside part of the garment for evaporation. This next-to-the-skin, long-sleeved garment is a great insulating layer under a jersey or jacket as well as a wear alone top for days when it will remain cool or you want protection from the elements.

There are also lightweight, hydrophobic, mesh-type tank tops that can be worn alone on hot days to give you some protection from the sun while still offering you a "tank-type" look. While not as much protection as a full jersey, a tank top is still better than no top if you fall. This base layer may also be used under a jersey for an extra lightweight, dry, insulating layer in cooler weather.

JACKETS AND OTHER OUTERWEAR

Quick-Tip: - Riding in the rain is potentially dangerous! Find a safe, dry place - like a pub - and wait it out!

The number one asked question about rainwear is whether or not you need a GoreTex™ type jacket. Our answer is, maybe. The term "GoreTex™'" is actually the trade name for a fabric developed by William Gore. It refers to a laminated fabric that leaves the finished product waterproof (up to a point,) windproof, and breathable. GoreTex™ has been used in shoes, tents, outerwear, and many other types of outdoor products as well as in cycling.

Our survey says that garments made of fabrics that are 100% waterproof, even with a myriad of well situated vents and touted to be "breathable", may not allow moisture to transfer outward quickly enough for cycling. Under normal spring, summer, and early fall temperatures - 45°-70°, even the most average rider is usually too fast to allow the water build-up from the inside of the garment to evaporate. Thus, the rider tends to get wet and stay wet, although probably not cold, until he or she stops riding.

One of the other problems with laminated products, especially rain jackets, is that continual folding and unfolding as you shove the garment in to a seat pack or handlebar bag, tends to crack the lamination and the fabric develops leaks. So much for waterproofness!

The number two question is, do I really need a jacket made specifically for cycling? Yes, if you plan to continue cycling. A cycling specific jacket is cut with longer sleeves and tail while the body is tapered to keep a close profile so the garment doesn't fill up with air. The longer sleeves stay put to protect your wrists and lower arms as you bend over the handlebars, and the longer tail keeps water from soaking your rear end and back as it flies up off the rear wheel. A cycling specific jacket should also be lightweight, well-ventilated, highly wind and water RESISTANT, and fairly vapor permeable.

A properly layered outfit topped off with a jacket like this, will afford a more comfortable ride. It will also allow inside moisture to evaporate at a reasonable rate, keep a light rainshower from soaking through, and protect from 90+% of the wind. The fabrics used to make these garments are either lightly coated or spun of very fine "microfilaments" that have been engineered to do exactly what they say they do. The fabrics are very rugged, wash and dry easily, and won't lose their inherent water and wind resistant properties.

Temperature range for a jacket like this is probably from 40°- 60°. And, the uses for a jacket with these many types of advantages range from golf to running, to cross-country skiing.

FINGERS, TOES, EARS, AND NOSE - FROSTBITE ZONES!

Quick-Tip for cold weather riding: If you find you are unable to tolerate cold weather riding without compromising your safety or dexterity, we have methods to allow you to train indoors.
(see: Indoor Training chapter)

Earlier on, we mentioned that keeping your head, neck, and upper body protected staves off heat loss. Fingers and toes often are the other areas that get cold, tingly, and finally force you off the bike to get circulation going again! Even moderately cold temperatures of +/-35° feel much colder at 15 or 20mph in a head wind.

EARS AND NOSES (how come it isn't earses and noses?)

We'll begin at the top. Helmets are absolutely MANDATORY! But, since we have an entire chapter on helmets, we'll talk about what to wear UNDER your helmet.

If your ears are sensitive to the cold there are thin, windresistant, yet breathable ear bands that won't squeeze your head or give you a headache but will keep your ears warm without interfering with your hearing. Ear bands take up virtually zero room in your pack and come in handy when the weather changes unexpectedly.

For colder weather, there is also the balaclava (no, no, not baklava, that's a Greek pastry!) It covers your entire head and neck and as much of your face as is practicable, without compromising your eyesight or breathing. You can actually pull it up over your mouth and nose so that you are warming the air you breathe and are not taking cold air directly into your lungs through your mouth and nose. This garment is especially important for those who tend to get cold and stay cold, have breathing difficulties such as asthma and allergies, and for those with thin or little hair.

Also for colder weather, but where there is no need for neck and face protection, there is a small "skull cap" that protects most of your head, excluding ears and neck. It is made of the same windresistant and breathable fabric as the ear bands and balaclavas detailed above.

FINGERS AND TOES(ES)

GLOVES

Keeping your hands comfortable while cycling isn't just about keeping them warm. Your hands can take a real beating during a bike ride. In a fall from your bike, the tendency is to put your hands out first. The pavement will not be kind to the delicate skin on your hands! Gloves help to protect your hands from scrapes, bruises, and cuts.

In addition, even the

person with the most perfect fit on his or her bike may experience problems such as pain and numbness in palms, fingers, wrists, and even up the arms and into the shoulders and neck. Any of these can be helped with a good pair of cycling gloves, although there is no substitute for a proper fit.

Most cycling gloves are "fingerless", meaning the fingers of the glove are cut off just below the second finger joint. This leaves the ends of your fingers uncovered offering you more dexterity with the brake and shift levers. Cycling gloves are commonly secured at the wrist with velcro to keep them snugly on your hand. The backs of the gloves are either a cotton-crochet mesh or lycra, allowing breathability, and often have a terrycloth area sewn over the forefinger and down towards the thumb. The palm, which may be covered in either a real leather or a synthetic fabric which is washable and stays fairly soft, is padded for comfort, cushion, and shock absorption. The padding may be made of foam or a shock absorbing gel.

Did you ever wonder what the terrycloth panel on your cycling gloves is for? Does your little nosey run when you ride?

How much and what type of padding becomes personal choice. For those riders with small hands, too much padding will bunch up in the palm, cause blisters, and may even make the glove so bulky that your fingers cramp up trying to grip the handlebars. Cycling gloves should fit VERY snugly without cutting off circulation to any part of your hand. If you find that using cycling gloves does not alleviate all the problems you have with your hands, it is time to go back to the drawing board and discover what is causing your discomfort.

Quick-Tip: When removing cycling gloves, peel them off like a banana, resulting in an inside-out glove. Trying to remove a wet

cycling glove by pulling on the ends of the finger areas, like a regular driving or dress glove, is futile AND frustrating! The gloves will be just fine!

As for keeping those little fingertips warm during colder weather, there are liners for under your existing gloves and full-fingered gloves of varying degrees of warmth. Remember NOT to sacrifice dexterity in favor of super warm, bulky gloves.

SOCKS AND OTHER FEET-ABLES

And, how about those little piggies, and the rest of your feet for that matter? Do they get really, really cold and numb, even in moderate temperatures? Or, do your feet perspire a lot, resulting in wet socks and shoes? Unhappy feet can be very unpleasant.

Even though it looks cool to ride without socks, it is NOT our recommendation. Un-socked feet can become cold,

itchy, sometimes smelly, and seriously unhappy feet! Here is one area where we recommend a NATURAL fiber – WOOL. The problem with most synthetics in your shoes is that the lining of your shoes do not breathe and the wicking properties of a synthetic will not know where to send the collected moisture. Wool has a "core" between the inner and outer parts of the fiber which traps the moisture and hangs on to it. Your feet stay dry and so do your shoes.

The wool socks we have found are VERY soft and do not shrink. They also are almost totally hypoallergenic and should not itch even the most sensitive skin. If, however, you are convinced that you are not able to wear wool, we can also recommend socks made from Coolmax™ mesh or Coolmax™ mesh combined with Kevlar™ reinforced heels and toes.

Quick Tip:
Make certain that you put
your shoes in a dry place

(not an oven or a microwave!) and stuff them with paper or use shoe trees if they get wet! This way they will retain their shape and not shrink

• •

A pair of small neoprene (the same fabric that is used in wetsuits,) digit-covers, will slip right over those socks and provide a little extra warmth and dryness for just your toes, if this is the area that is most affected by the cold.   If your entire foot does not like the cold, there are waterproof, windproof, and breathable over-the-sock liners. They will actually allow your feet to perspire a little while at the same time not permit this inside moisture to chill. Instead, a secondary barrier against the wet and cold elements is set up and your feet stay warm.

Finally, we have the ultimate foot and shoe protection (stay inside - just kidding!) There are several versions of an over-the-shoe neoprene booty that zips up the back. Most have a template molded into the sole so you can cut out the appropriate shape for the style of cleat you use. Or, you may leave them uncut if you do not use cleated shoes.

Of course, you can combine any or all of this to keep you cycling in all sorts of nasty weather. Our best advice is to experiment with different combinations until you are satisfied. Or, call, write, fax, or email!!!!! HUBBUB

Cycling Amenities
"Little Things Mean A Lot"
(Isn't that a Cole Porter song?)

Quick-Tip: Technical Accessories & Products Work!

It is so interesting how the lack of a little, seemingly insignificant item can make you so <u>MISERABLE</u>!

Ponder these questions for a moment:

• Does your skin easily sunburn or windburn?

• Are you prone to skin irritations, bladder, or yeast infections?

• Are you prone to leg cramps or foot cramps?

These are questions that should not come up after you are 30 miles out on the second day of a seven day tour! You need to be prepared for those difficulties which may not only irritate you but could potentially ruin an otherwise once-in-a-lifetime experience.

Problem: Sunburn/Windburn - Solution: Sun Block

Sunburn and/or windburn can be nasty and even outright dangerous. Sunblock products should be good for your skin, (we recommend sun and wind blockers that are aloe vera based.) Sunblock comes in various SPF strengths (skin protection factors,) as low as 4 to as high as 45. The higher the number, the more powerful the ultra-violet ray blocking capability and the less the burning and tanning effects. Even on an overcast day, UV rays can come and getcha'. Windburn will also dry out your skin no matter

1

what the conditions! Instead of a full makeup job in the mornings, a little of your regular moisturizer plus the appropriate strength Sunblock ought to do the trick. (Guys too!)

Problem:
Skin Irritations
Solution: Medicated
Chamois Cream

As for the more nasty problems of saddle sores, boils, or other skin irritations from the combination(s) of cycling shorts, pedaling, and moisture, we think that a **medicated chamois cream** formulated especially for cycling is the product best suited to soothe already unhappy skin as well as help to keep healthy bottoms healthy. In addition, a medicated cycling-specific cream will keep the chamois area of your cycling shorts soft, therapeutically lubricated, and free from excess moisture. Other remedies, such as A&D ointment, are good for your skin but tend to be absorbed too quickly and will not offer prolonged protection. Stay away from petroleum-based products such as Vaseline or K-Y. They are good water barriers but offer little else for human skin!

Problem:
Bladder, Yeast,
Bacterial Infections
Solution:
Your Own Medication(s)

If you know you are prone to yeast and bladder-type bacterial infections, bring medication along that works for you! Do not expect to walk into a local drug store in New Zealand or the Netherlands and find what you are used to seeing!

To help prevent these kinds of problems, make certain that your cycling shorts are VERY CLEAN - use a good quality cleaning agent that rinses clear. Also, dry your shorts inside-out to the air. Some folks take a clothes-pin (remember those?) and clip their not-quite-dry-yet shorts to the back of their rear rack or seat pack to dry on the road! You might also want to try a pair of the unpadded liners we talk about in our

Apparel chapter.

Problem:
Muscle Cramping
Solution:
Fluid Replacement
Drinks

Muscle cramping is a nasty problem! You can PREVENT it before it occurs!

Muscle cramps during exercise are the result of a build-up of lactic acid and a depletion of essential body fluids (electrolytes.). Oftentimes, you don't even realize how much fluid your body is using up until it is too late. We recommend that you begin supplementing just plain water with a fluid replacement drink product as soon as you hit 25 miles! Carry a second water bottle with you both while training and on tour or, if that is not possible, reload your bottle with the replacement fluid when you stop for a water refill.

Fluid replacement drinks should be easy to digest. By all means, try them out first - some have been known to create gas, and some seem to work better for women than men! - we don't know why. Most fluid replacement products are available in more than one flavor and many are offered in a one-bottle pre-measured dose that is easy to pack and carry with you on tour.

A Health Tip: If you are diabetic, fluid replacement drinks and energy bar supplements should be checked for their carbohydrate content!

Problem:
"Bonking"
Solution:
Food

Cyclists have a term we call "bonking." Literally, it means - "ran out of gas!" Cyclists also have the bad habit of not eating enough food until AFTER running out of gas. We are not claiming that you will lose weight on a cycling tour. However, you DO need enough energy to keep going until the end of the cycling day - every day.

While you might want to munch on fruit, granola, or whatever you find gives you

REAL energy (okay, an occasional candy bar and a soda might do!) there are now many types of energy bars available. Formulated especially for high calorie need situations, energy bars come individually wrapped, are easy to carry, and need no refrigeration. Make certain that you check the ingredients for those things to which you might be allergic (many are made with apples or nuts, for example,) and for fat, carbohydrate, and calorie content. Some are much more palatable than others, so EXPERIMENT with different types until you find a brand and flavor you like and that does the job.

Problem:
Protecting Your Eyes
Solution:
Wrap-Around
Sports Glasses

If you wear contact lenses, you know how it feels when even the tiniest speck of dirt gets in your eye - like a BOULDER! Wrap-around-style glasses with interchangeable lenses offer not only defense from stuff flying up off the road, but also protection from UV and Blue light rays from the sun! You can change to a low light lens for those monochromatic days (it adds contrast to everything,) or a clear lens for real early rides or when you find yourself just hitting dusk and everything begins to disappear. **In our opinion, protective eyewear is not a luxury - it is a necessity!**

For those who need to wear prescription glasses when they ride, there are special options for adding your prescription to sports eyewear. This is not an inexpensive alternative, but a very good, technical remedy for the sportsperson who will wear these glasses a lot. Your prescription will be able to "clip-in" behind the outer protective lens. This gives you a first class, optically correct result instead of a second class one.

Problem:
How Much Farther
Do I Have To Go?
Solution:
Cycling Computer

4

For training purposes, it is REALLY nice to know how fast and how far you are going. This way, you will know how long that 50 mile day on tour takes. Cycle computers can tell you everything from how fast you are turning your legs (cadence or RPM,) to how many inches you are traveling with each revolution of the wheels (gear ratio.) Do you need to know all that stuff? Probably not - but, speed, average speed, time of day, cumulative distance, and trip distance are all valuable features.

There are two basic types of cycling computers - wired and wireless. Both kinds run on long lasting batteries, utilize a head that looks like a watch face with digital read-outs, and have several buttons with which to change the various functions. The computer head clips onto a bracket on your handlebars.

Wireless units have a small transmitter/receiver that attaches to the top of your front fork. This sensor receives its information from a magnet attached to the front wheel. It then relays the signals to the head of the computer on your handlebars. Because of the nature of the transmitter-receiver system, cadence or RPM is not available on wireless units at this time - (you would need two transmitters/receivers and the signals would interfere with one another.) Also, wireless units are NOT recommended with the use of heart-rate monitors because of possible transmission interference.

Wired units work essentially the same way except that the transmitter (in this case, it is actually a magnet,) that is attached to your fork is connected to the computer head bracket via a cord or wire. There is still a magnet attached to the front wheel to relay signals. Those units that record cadence or RPM will have two wires that actually run toward the rear of the bike to pick up information from the crank (RPM) and rear wheel (all other signals.) Wired units are ordinarily less expensive than wireless. They also have more potential for failure due to the fragile nature of the wires themselves... (such as slamming them in car trunks or having a tree limb or stick rip through them while off road.)

Even the most basic unit will give you current speed, daily distance, and cumulative trip distance and costs around $25.00. What a nice way to pat-yourself-on-the-back for a good ride!

A final note about cycling computers: If you use an indoor trainer (see "Off-Season Training section,") you might want to purchase your cycling computer with a rear-mounting harness. The simple, mechanical indoor trainers work from your rear wheel; this means that you need rear sensors to pick up the information.

Problem:
I Need More Information
Solution:
Heart Rate Monitor

As an additional training aid, heart rate monitors actually let you know how YOU are doing. For anyone who has had heart problems or a treadmill-type stress test, you probably have used one of these units. The digital read-out unit is worn on your wrist like a watch, or may be clipped into a handlebar mounted bracelet. There are audible signals for different target heart-rate zones that can be programmed into the unit. A band is worn around your chest that contains the transmitters that send the signal of your heart rate to the watch. The heart monitors made today are VERY reliable.

As a training device, heart rate monitors can help you to increase your aerobic capacity, keep track of the time you spend in and out of your target heart rate zone, and let you know when you are having either a terrific day or a lousy one! There are very simple models that give you basic information and sophisticated units that have the capability of allowing you to download all the day's information into your personal desktop computer.

If you travel the same training course over and over and you sometimes wonder why you can accomplish the distance in a faster time some days than others, our research has shown that your performance capabilities are tied to a great many things. For example, what you eat, how well you sleep, what kind of stress you are experiencing, even whether you are angry or are catching a cold will all affect your performance on any given day.

Over time, feedback you get from the heart rate monitor, along with a history you might keep in a training log or diary, will begin to show you trends. Then, when you have an exceptionally good day or conversely a particularly lousy one, you might be able to trace the origins and see what worked or make adjustments for the future.

Problem:
What's Behind Me?

Solution:
Rear View Mirrors

While riding a bike, there may be an element of danger if you have to balance while trying to look over your shoulder or turn around to check what is coming up behind you. Here are the available solutions.

First is a handlebar-mounted mirror. If you have a straight-across style bar, the type found on hybrids or mountain bikes, there is a mirror that can be "plugged in" to the end of the bar. The mirror replaces the end plug and is on a flexible arm that pivots. The face of the mirror is about 3" in diameter and usually convex so that "objects in the mirror are closer than they appear." A second style mirror for a straight handlebar is almost identical except that it velcros in place, using a portion of the handlebar grip. (This can make the left hand grip feel bulky.)

Handlebar-mounted mirrors for 10 speed style bars use the same type mirror face and flexible arm attached to a metal clamp that fits over the left brake handle. They are then secured in place with a velcro strap. Again, you may experience a different feel on your left brake lever with this type of mirror attached.

The second solution is a mirror mounted to your helmet or eyeglasses. Helmet mirrors used to clamp to the outer shell of the old-style "hard shell" helmets with a little "C-clamp" device. Now, with the newer micro-shell helmets, these mirrors attach with a self-stick patch and velcro. The mirror is extended on a little arm and is fully adjustable.

Eyeglass mirrors are very similar to the helmet styles, but usually wrap-around the left temple of your glasses and are easily removed when not needed.

The problem we have found with helmet and eyeglass mirrors is actually a function of your eyesight. If you have trouble focusing at a distance of only a few inches, you may have a problem with this style mirror. Also, you may want to practice using the mirror in low or no traffic areas for a few miles. The tendency is to stare at the mirror and forget where you are riding!

NO-TECH

Quick-Tip: - Non-Technical Accessories Can Add To Your Fun!

What do you do when you go on vacation? TAKE PICTURES! of course.... So, have you tried one of the little "disposable" cameras? Believe it or not, they take great pictures, don't cost a lot, are lightweight, and easy to pack. You also do not need to worry about losing, breaking, or traveling with your very best Nikon.

If you still want to take your own camera equipment, talk with your tour company director about the use of a handlebar bag on the bicycle provided for your tour. This allows you to carry the camera in front of you as well as in a protective environment. Most handlebar bags can be retrofitted with foam that you can cut especially for your camera, lenses, filters, and film.

Caution: Loading up the front end of the bike with heavy items makes the steering characteristics of the bicycle change, especially going downhill. Practice riding with your equipment before you venture out on your tour.

What time is it? Made you look, huh? Well, I certainly don't recommend taking your Movado Museum watch on tour! There are many sport watches that are inexpensive, reliable, waterproof, easily set and reset, and have alarms and night lights. And, if you lose it, NO BIG DEAL!

Quick-Tip: - Better to be seen than heard (screaming!) or THERE'S NO SUCH THING AS TOO MUCH SAFETY! ALWAYS carry some form of identification with you - driver's license, or in the case of a trip overseas, your passport. Do not leave important personal belongings onthe bicycle in the handlebar or seat bag when you leave the bike to go to a bathroom, restaurant, or on a sightseeing excursion.

Occasionally you may find yourself on your bike at dusk with cars coming up behind you - uh oh! And, while there are several schools of thought on the to-be or not-to-be seen scenarios, OUR recommendation is THERE IS NO SUCH THING AS TOO MUCH SAFETY!

There is a simple and inexpensive solution to the getting-caught-with-your-lights-out situation... just flip the little switch on a reflector-cum-flashing light. These small, lightweight units have flashing LED's that work hundreds of hours on two AA batteries and can be seen for well over 1/2 mile. (Don't I wish I'd thought of this one?) Besides the models that can be used to replace your existing rear reflector, there are units that can be strapped to your arm or leg, attached to a helmet, or even clipped onto a belt or backpack.

Other more sophisticated lighting systems for those who want to light up the road in front of you and been seen by oncoming cars are available as well as a variety of reflective apparel and tapes that stick to everything from your shoes to your helmet. Much depends upon how much riding you do either at dawn, dusk, or late at night.

And, when you find yourself off your bike unexpectedly (as in - OOPS, I fell down,) there are a variety of small medical kits to carry with you. Or, you can always offer to help someone else who might need a Band-Aid. It is also comforting when you are traveling to have those things with which you are familiar when you are injured.

Quick Tip: Don't forget to carry emergency equipment such as a bee-sting kit if you have allergies or special medical needs.

(If you have a particular medical problem(allergies, heart condition, etc.) make certain you have the proper medical alert information with you.)

Problem:
Flat Tire
Solution:
Patch Kit, Extra Tube, Tire Levers, and Air

We highly recommend that you not be the one who gets a flat tire and then has to ask someone else for a pump or other inflation device, patch kit, extra tube, or a quarter to call AAA.

Quick Tips:

First rule to help prevent flats is to make certain that your tires are at maximum inflation. This prevents what we call "snakebite" or pinch-type flats, where the tube gets pinched between the wire beading that holds the tire onto the rim and the rim itself.

Second rule is to check the inside of the tire for thorns, glass, or anything

that might have caused the flat to begin with, before installing a brand new tube. (But, don't get cut doing it!)

There are now "glueless" self-adhesive patches available to fix an inner tube with a small, pinprick type hole in it. The trick to making them work is to put the patch on the VERY CLEAN spot, put the tube and tire back together, and immediately inflate the tube. The air pressure coupled with the pressure of the tube against the inside of the tire's sidewall, helps to set up the glue. If you are using regular style patches and glue, carry extra inner tubes anyway. Rubber cement patches should really sit up overnight for the glue to do a good job.

And, before you plunge a screwdriver into your brand new inner tube, learn the proper procedures to change a flat tire. Take some time to get to the bike shop and ask for a tire changing lesson. Then you can buy an extra inner tube and feel confident you know what to do with it

should you need it.

Quick Tip: This is a "you're lookin' good" tip: When you purchase that spare tube for your bike, tear the end-flap that shows the type and size inner tube you bought off the box, and stick it under the rubber band in which your tube was wrapped - this way, when you're out in nowheresville or you are in an unfamiliar bike shop without your wheels, you will know exactly what size and type tube you need!

Okay, you've fixed the flat, now let's see you get air back in that tire! Frame-mounted pumps are the tried and true, been-around-forever solution to getting air in a tube. But wait! There are new instant inflation devices that make this process a breeze. The ONLY drawback is that they use disposable, (non-reusable,) CO_2 cartridges. We think this is a small price to pay in making up for the effort it takes to get your tire pumped up to recommended pressure with a small frame pump - in many cases upwards of

100-110 pounds per square inch. (PSI)

These instant inflators can be regulated to allow in small amounts of air so that you can make certain your tire is staying on the rim. They can also be used to top off your tires just before you go out for a ride. (Which you should do EVERY TIME you ride.)

As for fixing other problems that might occur on your bike while you are on the road, there are a series of new, high-quality, compact all-in-one tools that include items such as tire levers, chain breaker, allen wrenches, and screwdrivers. These multi-purpose tools are easily packed and very convenient.

Organized, supported tours do have a technician available for any mechanical problems that might occur with your bike. Most of the time, the tour leader for the day is also well-qualified to assist with the average breakdown. Sometimes, however, you might have to wait for the repair van to come along to assist you.

It may just pay to have some working knowledge of a few of the minor problems that could go wrong on the road, such as having your chain fall off or having a wheel go out of true (meaning it may hit the brake shoes from side to side or hop up and down after hitting something.) If you want more in-depth knowledge of how to repair things such as broken chains or spokes, brake or derailleur adjustments, etc., we suggest you get a good maintenance manual or take a bicycle maintenance course.

IMPORTANT QUICK TIP:
In addition to knowing how to change a flat tire, it is imperative that you understand how quick-release wheels and the quick-release mechanisms for your brakes operate. Get a hands-on lesson from the bike shop! You should be familiar with removing and installing your wheels well enough to note at a glance if there is something askew.

Okay, so now you have a bunch of things to take with you - you can't just hold them in your hands! Some people are used to wearing a fanny pack. They work pretty well to carry small, lightweight items. However, to hold tools, an extra jacket, maybe an apple or sandwich, it may be helpful to have a clip-on or velcro-in-place pack tucked up behind your saddle. These packs come in a variety of shapes and sizes and, because they are carried over your rear wheel, will not create any problems due to excess weight.

HELMETS-R-YOU
You Mean, I Hafta' Wear A Helmet???

This is a subject with ZERO room for discussion on our part. Here are the Top Ten Reasons "Why I Don't Like To Wear A Helmet" heard over the last 20 years:

Number 10
Helmets are so ugly

Number 9
I'm a very defensive cyclist

Number 8
I'm only riding around the neighborhood

Number 7
Helmets are for sissies

Number 6
Helmets are too heavy

Number 5
Helmets are too hot

Number 4
Helmets give me a headache

Number 3
I can't find a helmet to match my bike

Number 2
Helmets give me helmet-hair

Number 1
Helmets are UN-COOL

Now, here are the top 10 reasons you should wear a helmet...

Numbers 10-9-8-7-6-5-4-3-2 and 1

NO ONE WANTS TO DISCONNECT YOUR LIFE-SUPPORT SYSTEM AFTER YOUR ACCIDENT!!!!!!

Not wearing a helmet while cycling is tantamount to not wearing a helmet while playing pro football. Today, a good cycling helmet weighs less than 8 ounces, is extremely well-ventilated, and when fit correctly, will actually feel as if you have nothing on your head! In really hot, sunny weather, a helmet will in fact, protect you from the sun. There is

HUB BUB

1

no question that a HELMET CAN SAVE YOUR LIFE! in case of an accident. (Also, your first set of skull x-rays in the hospital emergency room will cost 3-4 times as much as the helmet you should have been wearing!)

Even though the new-style helmets are very light, they meet incredibly stringent standards in all certified crash tests. Helmets are designed to absorb the impact of a fall and then break. Once you have hit the pavement with any force, it is prudent to replace your helmet, even if you are unable to see evidence of a break. Many helmets have "crash replacement" guarantees with a reduced re-purchase price to help ease the pain - both on your head and your wallet!

Quick Tip: For Washing Your Helmet. Prepare a mild solution of warm dishwashing soap and water in a bucket. Grab your helmet by its straps and dunk it up and down in the soapy water. Rinse it in clear water the same way and let it dry - out of the sun. The scuzziness will be GONE!

As with everything else that makes cycling safe and enjoyable, the fit of your helmet is most important. If you find you experience the "squeezing" effect of a misshapen or incorrectly sized helmet, some of our "Top 10 Reasons Why I Don't Like To Wear A Helmet" are probably true for you. All heads are NOT created equal, i.e. some heads are rounder and some are more oblong. It logically follows then that there should be differences in the interior shape of helmets. There are.

Even though they often just say small, medium, large, etc. on the outside of the packaging, helmets are also measured in centimeters and/or inches. A quick and easy method to find out what size you need is to take a tape- measurement above your eyebrows of the circumference of your head.

Determining which shape might be better for you is

done much the same way using a piece of thin cardboard (or something similar,) taping it together, carefully slipping it off, and looking at the shape. You can figure it out from here!

Adjustments to make certain that your helmet sits comfortably, securely and squarely on your head, level with your forehead, should be made with the helmet straps. If you are able to easily push the helmet back to expose all of your forehead and the front part of your hair, the fit is incorrect. Either readjust the straps, the inside fit pads, or try a differently shaped and sized helmet.

HELMET ACCESSORIES

When you buy your helmet, allow a little extra room for a headband, earband, or even a thin head-covering when the weather gets cooler. If you perspire unmercifully, terry headbands will help to mop your brow and keep the perspiration from running into your eyes.

The cold-weather accessories, including earbands, balaclavas, and skull-caps are usually made of windresistant fabrics and have many uses besides cycling. (Check out the apparel section for a better description of these.)

Many people use a small rear-view mirror that velcros onto the outer shell of the helmet. These mirrors take a little getting used to, but are indispensable for those who do not like to turn around or look over a shoulder for traffic. If you find your eyesight is unable to get used to this type of mirror, there are also handlebar mounted models available. (see the Amenities Section.)

There are a few helmets made with visors. Some are detachable and some are not. A removable helmet visor that secures with velcro is also available. It will retro-fit most of the newer micro-shell helmets. If you have one of the older, hard shell helmets, think about trading it in for something 1/2 the weight and twice as well ventilated - then, you can add the visor, too!

Try to buy a set of replacement pads for the insides of your helmet. You will find that eventually, you can't even wash the scuzziness away! And, an extra pad kit may also come in handy if you bought your helmet with one hair style and decide to make a major change the next season.

A final word about helmets - set a good example for children, as well as adults who don't see the need for protecting their heads when they ride. Wear your helmet EVERY TIME you get on your bike, even when just pedaling to the corner store! It only takes a split-second for an accident to occur. HUBBUB

WRONG   RIGHT

CYCLING SHOES AND CLIPLESS PEDALS
"They're Made For Walkin' - Too!"

Just as cycling shorts will offer you many advantages, a good pair of cycling shoes, especially coupled with a set of clipless pedals, will enhance your riding comfort and pedaling capabilities.

Cycling shoes are different from any other athletic shoe because they have a special stiff sole that does not allow the bottom of the shoe to bend upwards. This in turn gives you a positive "platform" upon which to pedal.

We are not suggesting that you run right out and get a special cycling shoe; but, if you find that on longer rides, your feet either fall asleep or burn, cycling shoes will probably go a long way to solving the problem.

The "feet that fall asleep" syndrome is especially noticeable among those who use toe clips and straps. The tendency is to jam your feet into the end of the toe clip as you pedal. This causes your toes to hurt and eventually fall asleep. The other problem - "burning" feet - usually occurs after long rides and is also caused by an inappropriate shoe, or shoe, clip, and pedal combination.

A cycling shoe does not fit like a running shoe nor does it feel like a "normal" shoe. The stiff sole tends to rock you back on your heels slightly. Cycling shoes should fit snugly, still be comfortable while walking, and give you room to wiggle your toes.

Quick-Tip: Buying your cycling shoes with a little extra room allows for your feet to swell while riding. Also, you will be able to use a thicker sock for cooler weather

GOING CLIPLESS

For decades, racing cyclists and cycling enthusiasts used a pedal, shoe, and cleat combination in conjunction with toe clips and straps as a means to better efficiency. The system worked pretty well, as did horses and buggies before airplanes! (Is that distinct enough?)

With the exception of indexed shifting, clipless pedal and shoe systems are the single most important new advance in cycling in many, many years. The idea comes from downhill ski boot-and-binding technology. The pedal contains a spring-clip type mechanism that clips around the cleat, which is fastened to the sole of the shoe. When engaging the pedal, you will ordinarily hear an audible "click" and, voila' - you are in!

Some people think that "in" means "locked in." Au contraire! Once practiced and understood, exiting from a clipless pedal is a simple twist of your foot. In our opinion, a novice rider who starts with the clipless system, will be miles ahead of the cyclist who still uses toes clips and straps. We highly recommend that you practice using your clipless pedal system on an indoor training device for a period of time until you are confident that you get the sense of how it all works. This way, you won't come to that first stop sign and fall over like the little guy on the tricycle used to do on "Laugh In."

Here are several technical advantages to a clipless system:

• Your feet will always be in the appropriate position over the pedals, giving you the most power from your pedaling stroke.

• You will become much better at pulling up with one foot while the other is pushing down, creating a smoother, less choppy circle (that is the point, actually.)

• This pulling and pushing motion will, after some practice, make you much more efficient with less waste of energy resulting in less fatigue.

• This pushing and pulling motion will also train and develop your muscles to work appropriately for cycling.

• You will be able to pedal over the same terrain in a higher gear, creating less strain on your system and once again adding to your efficiency.

• Some people have even said the degree to which your pedaling efficiency is increased may be as much as 20%!

RECREATIONAL CYCLING SHOES

Okay, we haven't convinced you that you are ready for a clipless system. And, you are experiencing some problems with your feet. We're one step ahead of you. (Catching on to these terrible puns yet?)

Many of the cycling shoes that are made for use with the clipless systems are ride-ready without cleats. The cleats, which actually come with the pedals not the shoes, may be added later by removing a plug in the bottom of the shoe. (The cleat is actually recessed into the sole of the shoe so you do not walk on it.)

Now, you have a good quality cycling shoe in which you are able to walk when not riding. The stiff sole will fend off fatigue and the shape of the shoe will fit nicely into a double mountain-style nylon toe clip. We might also recommend a half-clip for those who just do not want the "cage" type system on their pedals. A half clip only covers the forward part of your foot, positions your foot correctly on the pedal each time you ride, and still gives you some modicum of pulling power. HUB8UB

Quick-Tip: No matter what type of shoe-pedal system you are using, if you have lace-up shoes, make certain that your laces are tucked away so they do not get caught in the chain or on the crank chainrings and cause you to fall.

Quick Tip, too: Always wear socks while riding. They will help to preventing that "burning" feeling as-well-as keep your feet dry.

WHAT TO TAKE
These days, less is more!
So, it follows that if you take the right
stuff You will not need more stuff.
Did you follow that?

Packing for a cycling tour does not have to be a complicated process. Many Tour Directors will send along a list of recommended apparel and accessories when you sign up for one of their tours.

Some companies routinely offer items such as helmets, water bottles, handlebar bags, and rear luggage racks for your use as part of their tour packages. Others rely upon you to bring many or most of these things in addition to your clothing and toiletries.

Here are some things to cogitate:

- Take into consideration the length of time you will be traveling - both on the bike and all the other vacation days.
- Find out how your luggage will be transported from day-to-day.
- Try to keep your belongings in one bag.
- Make certain that your personal things are easily identified.
- How often you will need to wash things such as undergarments, shorts, jerseys, and socks.
- Take more socks than you think you will need.
- Take your own washing agent if you have sensitive skin.
- Know what to expect under normal weather conditions as-well-as unusual weather for the region(s) you will be visiting.

- Consider spending the extra money for a really good, versatile wind/rain cycling-specific jacket that folds into its own rear pocket. It's worth it!

- Take more socks than you think you will need (yes, this is a repeat!)

- Bring those things that you know you will not be able to duplicate elsewhere at your destination.

- Prescription medications

- Personal toiletries such as tampons, toothpaste, deodorant, and makeup

- Your own saddle

- You own helmet

- Your own shoes and pedals

- Fluid replacement drinks and energy bars

- Check to see if you need more than just a passport for your destination(s).

- Check for immunization requirements for areas such as Asia or Africa.

- Indulge yourself small items such as pre-wrapped towelettes, mints and candies, or small, throwaway packs of dental floss.

We are assuming (rightly or not,) that you are NOT taking an extended tour that requires you to carry your own sleeping bag, tent, provisions, and cooking utensils. These month-long or more adventures, require a different kind of planning than the average leisure tour. Contact us for information about these types of tours. HUB HUB

SAMPLE SUITCASE
(seven day tour)

Here is a sample assortment for a 7-day tour: (adjust accordingly for different length adventures.)

- 3 pair good quality shorts, make certain you have ridden extensive miles in them or exactly the same type before your trip. You want no surprises in this area!
- 2-3 pair unpadded, seamless, long-legged, cycling specific undershorts
- 3 good sports bras (gender specific)
- 4-5 tops or jerseys - preferably not all cotton
- 1-2 base layers - sleeveless or long sleeve
- 7-8 pair cycling socks (We're telling you - you will be happy you listened to us.)
- cycling shoes (if you use them) and an extra pair of laces if necessary
- your pedals
- your saddle
- your helmet
- 1 good pair of walking/dining shoes (unless your cycling shoes are comfortable AND stylish!)
- 1-2 good pair of slacks for dinner
- 1-2 skirts and blouses or dresses
- 1 good wind/rain jacket
- 1 pr. arm warmers and leg warmers or
- 1 pr. tights
- whatever you prefer to sleep in
- small first-aid kit
- small tool kit
- disposable cameras (this way you won't forget to buy film!)
- sports watch
- your toiletries
- your medications
- your passport and a good place to carry it on your person while riding
- a fanny pack or under- seat bag that is easily removed
- extra plastic bags in which to put wet socks or, whatever!

• The 2 Minute Bicycle Safety Check • How To Train • Off-Season Training • A Typical Day On Tour •

THE TWO MINUTE SAFETY CHECK
(Don't Leave Home Without It!)

You do not have to be a master technician to perform a quick safety check each time you go to ride your bicycle. Oftentimes, you are tired when you return from a ride and don't remember that you've patched a tube, broken a spoke, or had some other small mechanical mishap on your last ride. You jump on your bike and take off only to have the tube go flat 100' down the road. BUMMER!

It is also imperative that YOU take the responsibility to learn the simple things about your bicycle that will keep you safe. EVERYONE is capable of doing these 10 quick-check things.

1. Measure the **air pressure** in both tires each time you ride.
   - the recommended pounds per square inch (psi) is actually printed on the sidewall of your tire.
   - keep your tire pressure to maximum for road riding – this will help prevent "pinch" flats and give you maximum shock resistance against bent rims.

2. Check to make certain that your **quick release levers** on your wheels are properly adjusted for tightness and in the closed position.

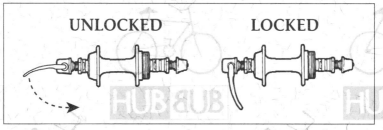

UNLOCKED   LOCKED

3. Check to make certain that your **quick release levers for your brake calipers** are closed – especially if you removed your wheel(s) the last time you rode.

4. Spin your wheels one-at-a-time to make certain they are straight or true and that they are not hopping up and down or hitting the brake shoes from side-to-side – if that is the case, have your wheels trued at a bike shop.

5. Make certain that your **handlebars and handlebar stems** are tight. Nothing is worse than having your handlebars suddenly rotate while you are leaning on them.

6. Make certain that your saddle is tight – same reason as above.

7. Take identification and some money with you.

8. Check to see if you have a patch kit, extra inner tube, pump or instant inflator and tire changing equipment with you.

9. Don't forget your helmet – make certain the straps are properly adjusted.

10. Give your bicycle a quick look for anything unusual – eventually you will notice even the smallest thing out of place.

HOW TO TRAIN
(On The Road)

There are those who show up for a bicycle tour with no training whatsoever, perhaps thinking that 35 miles is not very far to ride. At 55 mph in the car, that's true! But, we would hate to think that you were the one who wimped out and rode in the SAG wagon after the first 10 miles each day!

We know that by now, you're on the right size bike, wearing the proper clothing, and you've probably even picked a destination. We also know that if you ride your bicycle at about 10 miles per hour, you will accomplish the day's 35-50 mile ride in about 4-6 hours; this includes stopping for breaks and lunch.

Here are a few suggestions to get you in shape:

• try to get out and ride at 2-4 times per week, at least an hour at a time, for a couple of months before your trip.

• Ride the same course regularly so you can assess how you are improving. Include some hills and straighaways.

• Gradually increase your time in the saddle until you can ride for 2 or more hours each outing.

• Contact a local touring club and join one or two of their rides per week.

• Most touring-cycle clubs offer several "level of ability" rides when they go out, often A, B, and C.

- The "A" riders are the fastest and ordinarily go the furthest - sometimes up to 75 or 80 miles at a time. C riders are usually the "novice" or shorter distance, slower speed cyclists.

- We have found that most local cycling clubs are very friendly to new riders and welcome them on their rides.

- Sign up for a couple of organized day rides (25 or more miles) prior to your departure.

- These rides are "supported" with rest/food stops and have SAG wagons on the road to scoop you up if you break down or cannot finish.

- Riding with groups of people will help you with your bike handling skills as well as offer you company and a feeling of safety.

If you have any questions or would like more in-depth training information, there are several excellent training guides available. Just give us a call, or send a fax or email! HUB aUB

OFF-SEASON TRAINING
(Going Nowhere Fast!)

You need to train during the "off-season" - and, if you are stuck inside as we are here in Cleveland for several months of the year - an indoor trainer that utilizes your bicycle (instead of the stationary bike at the health club,) is as close to riding outside as you can get. A magnetic resistance trainer, (which is the type we recommend,) allows you to change gears while pedaling as well as giving you several optional resistance settings, each making it increasingly more difficult to pedal. You can hook your bicycle up to it in 15 seconds and it is quiet enough to watch TV or listen to music while you are pedaling away!

Since the rear end is elevated when it is attached to the trainer, we suggest a phone book or a device called a trak-blok that cradles your front wheel and levels the front end of the bicycle so that you do not feel as if you are riding downhill all the time. Don't forget that if your cycling computer gets its information from the front wheel, you may need to change to a rear mounting harness when using an indoor trainer!

Quick Tip: Protect the top tube and handlebar section of your bicycle with a towel or a "sweat net." Since there is no wind to dry you off while riding indoors, perspiration will drip onto your bicycle and can rust parts!

We know that many people run and swim in addition to cycling but, on those days when there is enough snow, off-season training might include cross-country skiing. This is a great counter-seasonal aerobic activity that will help keep your cardiovascular system in good shape as well as your arms and legs. The upper body movements will also serve to keep your arm, shoulders, and back muscles supple and developed.

Finally, don't overlook the benefits of a good massage therapist! Even if you are not injured, a good massage will help you to relax when you are not exercising and keep your muscles in shape.

When a new cycling season rolls around, you should be ready!

KEEPING TRACK - of you!!!!

We talked about cycle computers and training, we mentioned how much we greatly encourage the use of a **training diary or log**. Keep track of all of your activities including your training miles, how many hours you sleep, even your heart rate and what you eat. This type of ongoing information will help you to understand how your body is functioning on any given day.

And finally, a detailed record of your off-season training will give you a foundation of information to begin the season – it may put you miles ahead of other riders.

A TYPICAL DAY ON TOUR
(No SAGging)

We promise that you will be able to take a cycle tour and have a good time, if you are willing to get some practice in first. While 35 miles of riding per day may sound like a lot, think of it this way:

If you ride your bicycle at 8-10 miles per hour, you will cover a 35 mile tour day in 4-5 hours.

Here is what a typical tour day might look like:

7:00-7:30am
rise, shower, and dress

7:30-7:45am
pack up your stuff

7:45-8:15am
breakfast

8:15-8:30am
do 10-15 minutes of stretching

8:30am
check out your gear and get on the road (your tour tech probably checked your bike; it doesn't hurt to do your own 2 minute check yourself!)

10:00am
take a break, drink some fluids - it's been 1 ½ hours, so you've already covered 30-40% of the day's ride

10:30am
get back on the road and enjoy the scenery

Noon
stop for lunch and a longer rest - you've already covered 75% of the day's ride

1:00pm
back on the road for the last few miles

2:00-3:00pm
You did it! you've arrived at your destination - stretch, take a quick shower, get a snack, do

some sightseeing, meet some locals, take a nap, and be ready for a great dinner followed by a good night's sleep!

So, now how do you get to these amazing mileage totals? PRACTICE! Even if you are a great tennis player, golfer, swimmer, or runner, **nothing replaces road miles but road miles!** The muscles that are most essential for cycling, especially the quadriceps in your thighs, are rarely worked efficiently during any other exercise.

As with any other sport, begin slowly and build up to extended time and distance. (Read our How To Train chapter.) Stretch before each ride and learn about your limitations. Try not to have wild expectations about yourself and your abilities - be realistic. And, most of all HAVE FUN! HUB BUB

All The Print That's Fit To Read (Get Linked, Too!)

This section is really about all types of resources - not just destinations, or technical manuals, but information about worldwide weather, currency exchanges, etc. Much is available to you via the Internet and the World Wide Web. If you are "connected," you can get travel tips, weather information, and currency exchange rates right up until the day you depart. *For a good source of electronic information, visit the HubBub website at www. HubBub.com.*

The written word, however, still holds special value for us. Because we believe that there is probably no such thing as too much good information - (of course, the operative here is good,) we have listed a series of "topic" sections with just a few of the titles we have found most helpful or interesting in each. These are by no means the only resources for specific information and, should these selections not suffice, or you do not see a topic that covers your interest(s), please use the method with which you are most comfortable to contact us and we will compile another list of resource materials for you.

When you book a tour, your tour company director will send you a packet of information. In addition to those things that apply directly to the tour you have chosen, such as itinerary, expected weather, etc., there is often a bibliography of interesting books and other reference material for those who enjoy doing research before a trip.

Finally, new titles and other interesting information become available almost daily. Please feel free to contact us for updates about destinations, specific trips, equipment, or information you might need and are unable to locate.

Bon Voyage!

Very Partial Book List

The "Best Rides" Series - Books concentrate rides in the United States. There are more than 100 titles available. Call us for details!

These are well-researched little books that detail between 20 and 25 tours, on road and off, in different areas around the country. Levels of difficulty, detailed maps, and interesting places to stop are usually included. These types of rides offer you the opportunity to get a variety of riding experiences without doing the research! Just let us know the area in which you are interested.

Foreign Travel Books

While we do not have access to every country, or every region within a country, we will do our best to track down out a specific area for you. Some of the more popular titles are:

- Cycling France
- Cycling Canada
- Cycling Europe
- Europe By Bike
- Backroads of Holland
- Cycling Japan
- Bicycle Touring in Australia
- China by Bike

Maintenance Manuals
(abbreviated list)

Basic Maintenance and Repair - *Rodale Press*
Bicycle Repair Book - *Rob Van der Plas*
Fundamentals of Bicycle Repair - *VIDEO*
Mountain Bike Emergency Repair -
  Rob Van der Plas
Zinn & the Art of Mountain Bike Maintenance -
  Leonard Zinn

Books For New Bike Owners

The HubBub Guide to Cycling *(tee hee!)*
New Bike Owner's Guide - *Rodale Press*
600 Tips for Better Bicycling - *Rodale Press*

Training Guides

The Heart Rate Monitor Book - *Edwards*
   (helps to have a heart rate monitor)
Serious Training for Serious Athletes - *Burke*
Fitness Cycling - *Carmichael & Burke*
Stretching - *Anderson*
A Woman's Guide to Cycling - *Weaver*
Velo News Training Diary - *Velo Press*
Nutrition for Cyclist's - *Rodale Press*

Fun Books

Tales from the Bike Shop -
   Hershon (GREAT fun!)
Half Wheel Hell - *Hershon (more GREAT fun!)*
Cycle History - *Rob Van der Plas*
An Intimate Portrait of the tour de France
   (coffee table quality!)
The American Bicycle - *Hurd & Pridmore*

Books for Children
(these are imports and do not portray the use of helmets)

Friends - *Heine*
Mrs. Peachtree's Bicycle - *Silverman*
Little Red Riding Hood - *Ernst*

FIBER TECHNOLOGY

Bosui technology is a 3-part stretch laminate that is rated very high for waterproofness and breathability. Terrific weatherproofness with a single lightweight and compact layer. Nylon/polyurethane/ polyester.

Coretech/Coretech Flat/Coretech Mesh Fabric is constructed with a series of macro-micro yarns arranged from the inner to outer surface. The bulkier inner yarn transports perspiration quickly to the fine denier outer yarn creating a cool, dry environment. 100% colorfast polyester.

Cordura/Lycra combines the strength of cordura and resilience of lycra. A highly abrasion resistant material that is several times more crash resistant than nylon/lycra. 88% nylon cordura, 12% lycra.

Drycell is a soft, stretchable knit designed to be worn next to the skin. The fibers are exposed to a hydrophillic treatment that chemically changes the structure to enhance moisture movement. 80% polyester, 20% lycra.

Entrant G2 is a micro porous coating that blocks out wind and rain while allowing vapour to dissipate freely. Engineered to withstand stress, abuse and repeated washings without losing performance. 100% fade resistant polyester.

Stretch Entrant is a mechanical 4 way stretch version of above. This does tend to be less waterproof, but maintains the windblock and vapour permeable functions. 100% polyester.

ESP Mesh is a high memory yarn that provides stretch without lycra. Lightly brushed on the inside with moisture management properties, it is designed to be worn next to the skin. 100% polyester.

Fieldsensor quickly absorbs perspiration from the inner layer and pushes it to the outer surface where it evaporates. This capillary action is caused by a graduated fiber structure that increases in size from the inner to outer layer. highly functional under any exertion. 100% colorfast polyester.

Fieldsensor with Lycra quickly absorbs perspiration from the inner layer and pushes it to the outer surface where it evaporates. This capillary action is caused by a graduated fiber structure that increases in size from the inner to outer layer. Highly functional under any exertion. 85% polyester, 15% lycra.

Scotchlite is the basis of all Sugoi Hi Beam products. A reflective transfer film or tape that greatly enhances nighttime visibility.

Microfine is a light weight micro denier yarn, which through weaving and finishing, yields a fabric that is inherently water resistant and windproof, yet highly breathable. It's silky hand is treated to be anti-static in most environments. 2.9 oz. micro fibre polyester

Technifine is a revolutionary moisture transfer system. The micro-fibre technology is accelerated with a series of open channels that enhance absorption and force evaporation to the outer surface. It is the ultimate next to the skin performance fabric for high output activities.

Subzero is a beefy poly/lycra blend that is brushed on the inner side to provide excellent warmth and wicking properties. Treated for moisture movement. 80% polyester 20% lycra.

Versatech is a 2.9oz polyester superfine microfiber yarn, which through weaving and finishing, yields a fabric system that inherently makes it water resistant and windproof with exceptional breathability. 100% colorfast.

DEHYDRATION WARNING SIGNS

Most active people have experienced mild dehydration without knowing it. This is because the signs of mild dehydration can be subtle. As a body becomes more depleted of vital fluids, the warning signs become more obvious and the health risk more serious. To improve your performance and avoid heat illness, tune in to your body's warning signs of dehydration:

Warning Signs	What It Means
FATIGUE	While fatigue can be brought on by many factors, it can also be the first sign that the body is running low on fluids.
DIZZINESS AND LIGHT-HEADEDNESS	Dehydration reduced blood pressure and blood flow to vital organs.
MUSCLE CRAMPS	The first indication of severe dehydration, this signals excess loss of fluids, sodium and electrolytes due to profuse sweating.
NAUSEA	Irritation in the small intestine develops due to lack of fluids.
HEADACHES	As blood flow continues to decrease, so does the supply of fluids and oxygen to the brain.
COLD, CLAMMY SKIN	The body attempts to conserve fluids by decreasing circulation to the skin.
INABILITY TO SWEAT	The body's cooling system has virtually shut down because of the lack of fluids. This is an indication of heat stroke and medical attention should be sought immediately before loosing consciousness.

Julie Walsh, M.S., R.N.

STRETCHING EXERCISES FOR CYCLING

LOOSEN UP!
Beat knee pain by stretching. As far as patella pain is concerned, there is good evidence to suggest that tight hamstrings, quadriceps, calf muscles or ilio-tibial tract contribute to the knee pain. In some cases, having just one of these tissues tighter than it should be will be enough to cause pain in and around the knee cap. Good stretching will help lengthen them, so try stretching and compare with the healthier leg.

CALVES
Lean against a wall or chair and put your left foot flat on the floor. Move the left knee towards the wall - the stretch should be felt in your left calf. Then change to your right side.

HAMSTRINGS
Sit on a chair or the floor with your back supported and left leg out straight. Pull the left ankle and toes up and then lean your body forward and bow your head. The stretch will be felt at the back of the knee, thigh and possibly along the spine. Change to the right.

QUADS
Lie on the floor and bend your knee so that the heel moves to the buttock. Hold your left foot with your left hand and pull towards the buttock. The stretch should be felt at the front of the thigh. The alternative way is to use a friend. But take care not to tip your trunk forward, or the stretch will be lost. Change to the right.

ILIO LIBIAL TRACT
Sit on the floor, upright, with the right arm supporting you. Cross your right leg over the left and tuck it into the outside of the knee. The left arm then pulls the right knee and thigh over. The stretch will be felt on the outside of the right thigh and hip. Then change over.

MICHAEL J. CALLAGHAN, M.Phil., Grad. Dip. Phys. MCSP SRP
Chartered Physiotherapist: Great Britain Olympic Team 1988, 1992, 1996
England Commonwealth Games Team 1986, 1990, 1994
Honorary Physiotherapist British Cycling Federation

HUB&UB